Soul Healing
& Spirit Dancing

AF485252

Soul Healing
& Spirit Dancing

A SEASONAL JOURNEY TO EMBODY THE BALANCE, PEACE AND JOY THAT IS YOUR BIRTHRIGHT

Angela Kittock

MOONDANCE

Minneapolis, MN

Moondance Wellness Coaching

www.moondancecoaching.com

Copyright © 2023 by Angela Kittock.

All rights reserved. No part of this publication may be reproduced, distributed or transmitted in any form or by any means, including photocopying, recording, or other electronic or mechanical methods, without the prior written permission of the publisher, except in the case of brief quotations embodied in critical reviews and certain other noncommercial uses permitted by copyright law.

For permissions requests, contact the publisher at angela@moondancecoaching.com.

Quantity sales. Special discounts are available on quantity purchases by corporations, associations, and others. For details, contact the publisher at the email address above.

Soul Healing & Spirit Dancing/ Angela Kittock —1st edition.

ISBN 979-8-9889043-0-4 (paperback)

To the overworked and overwhelmed who know there is more to life than this. May your journey of finding balance, feeling better, and awakening to the deeper levels of your soul and spirit begin here.

Contents

PART IV: WINTER

FINAL WORDS

AUTHOR'S NOTE

The practices and ideas in this book have helped me tremendously in my journey of healing both body and soul. Embodying these practices has put the power of healing back into my own body, mind, heart, soul and spirit, where it should be, so I don't have to feel exclusively reliant on others. But I haven't done it all alone and at times I have worked with doctors, therapists, coaches and healers, and still do. Know yourself and know when it might benefit you to reach out for additional support. This book isn't meant to be a replacement for a comprehensive healing plan, but one important piece of it that focuses in particular on the soul and spirit. Getting examined by a physical or mental health professional is an excellent way to gain additional information; please utilize that tool as well. Use every tool in your toolbox! There's no shame in the healing journey, and working with others can be a powerful experience. Be discerning, trust your inner wisdom, and know who and what is right for you.

"MOONDANCE"

One day she realized she was tired of playing small.
She decided it was her time to shine.
There is no perfect moment, they'd always told her.
She smiled now and thought: no, THIS is the perfect moment. I am ready.
She felt a spark in every bone of her body, and a longing in her heart.
So she conjured up her courage and she stepped outside; she began to dance her joy for all the world to see.
She twirled and she glowed and she felt more alive than she ever had before.
She was radiant in that moment, as inner merged with outer.
Bathed by the light of the moon.

—ANGELA KITTOCK, 2017

Peace and Ease

IN MY WORK AS A SPIRITUAL life and wellness coach, I always have clients fill out an extensive intake form that covers body, mind, heart, soul and spirit. And do you know one of the main themes that comes up again and again as to why people are seeking out this kind of coaching? It isn't the desire for some kind of elaborate plan to transform and overhaul one's entire life; it's the simple but very real goal of wanting to *feel better*.

Whether it's stress and overwhelm, burnout and fatigue, anxiety and agitation, or a lack of pleasure and fulfillment in life that finally drives one to seek out support, everyone's got a valid reason for simply wanting to feel better. I think there is a deeper part of us that knows that balance, peace and joy aren't just a "nice to have" in our lives, they are essentials – in fact, they are *our birthright*.

A second theme that comes up again and again is wanting some form of guidance for the journey, whether it's a nudge in the right direction, a way to honor beginning a new phase of life, or simply a trusted voice for some accountability, support, and someone to bring you back to your own wise inner knowing when those other critical inner voices get a little too loud.

So, this book, too, has a simple goal: to help you discover that elusive sense of peace, joy and balance that has perhaps gone missing from your life, guide you to awaken to the deeper levels of your soul and spirit, and in the end, to support you in simply *feeling better*.

Peace and Ease

When I wanted to feel better in my own life, and shift out of the seemingly endless feeling of stress and struggle, I asked for one thing: *to feel a sense of peace and ease.* And you know what? That's actually what I got. But I'm going to bring you in on a little secret that I learned along the way: peace and ease are not entirely dependent on our external circumstances. As much as we like to think that peace, ease, joy, and that ever-elusive idea of balance, will come our way once we get the dream job, move to the ideal geographic location, or find that perfect new relationship – unfortunately it's just not the case.

When the world pandemic swept across the planet in 2020, I think most of us assumed that peace, ease, joy and balance would naturally return to our lives once we stopped wearing face masks, scavenging for toilet paper, and feeling like our lives had become some wild sci-fi thriller. And yet, here we are, facing whatever the next personal or world calamity may be, and still waiting. Waiting for our sense of peace and ease. Why hasn't it shown up yet?

Because you are still you. Now, don't get me wrong – you are an amazing being. I see you and your splendid gifts. But, if your sense of peace and ease is based entirely on external circumstances, you will forever be stuck in the pursuit of happiness. You can keep changing the container you're in hoping that you'll feel differently on the inside – and you will feel better temporarily! But if you're tired of constantly being in the pursuit of happiness, tired of the chase, tired of always needing the next perfect thing – then it's time to take back your power and learn to embody a sense of peace and ease that you can carry with you no matter what your life throws at you.

The good news? It doesn't matter how chaotic or dramatic the world or your life is right now – and with the way the world's been the last few years, there's a good chance it's both chaotic *and* dramatic – if what you desire to feel inside is a deep and lasting sense of peace and ease, then you have that option available to you, right now.

That Pivotal Moment

Let me bring you back to a time in my life when I was NOT experiencing peace and ease. Even after a decade has passed, I still remember this particular moment so vividly. I was 29 years old, standing at my kitchen sink in our rental house with its freakish lime green kitchen walls. I was washing my juicer for the umpteenth time while spending that summer trying to cure myself of Crohn's disease by exclusively consuming fresh juice - one of many endless attempts to rid myself of this disease that was wreaking havoc on my body and soul. I looked around at the numerous bottles and jars of supplements and tinctures stacked around the kitchen counter, the brown bags full of magic potions and pills lining the entryway. I saw my endless to-do list open on my laptop, staring at me menacingly from the kitchen table. Somehow, it was never finished and only managed to get longer. And I noticed a distinct feeling that life had become heavy and difficult and not very fun.

I wondered when this had happened. When you're a little kid you can't wait to become a grown-up and do whatever you want all the time! But somewhere along the way, life had instead become an endless to-do list and a myriad of health issues. This was a rather mundane moment, but it became pivotal for this single reason: I realized with certainty that something was wrong and I knew that it had to change.

We can go for days, weeks, even decades pretending that everything is fine on the surface. Maybe we're not even pretending – maybe we're simply asleep. Asleep to the possibility that our life could be different, that we deserve for it to be better, that there are other possible realities available to us aside from the one we're currently "living."

Asleep, because to wake up and look around at the reality we find ourselves in...is painful. But nothing changes if we stay asleep. We end up choosing an entire lifetime of mediocrity in order to avoid one painful moment of waking up to our reality, and realizing with utmost certainty – *my god, something needs to change*. In that moment, I knew with certainty that I was not okay carrying on in this way, slowly being crushed by the weight of the world. I craved peace and ease and I was determined to find it.

The Radical Step

In the decade that followed that pivotal moment, I began an ever-deepening journey of getting out of my own way, living in alignment with my true self, and awakening to the fullest and most empowered expression of who I am – so that my life felt lighter, flowed easier, and kept the flame lit on that once-missing spark of childhood wonder and magic.

The first few steps I took after that moment were huge in changing the way I felt about my life. Keep in mind that my life externally remained the same for a while – the Crohn's disease was still in and out of remission; I worked a job I didn't really care about; and I spent more time borrowing travel guides on Hawaii from the library than I did actually traveling anywhere.

But I kid you not, it was during this very time that I finally tasted my peace and ease. Why? Well, instead of continuing to push and force and control, I took the radical step of doing something I had never done before – I learned *how to do less*. For someone who had always considered themselves a perfectionist, I assure you, this was new territory.

First, I signed up for an 8-week Mindfulness Based Stress Reduction course. This was amazing. I had always hated meditating because I found it so physically uncomfortable that I couldn't even begin to enjoy whatever mental benefit was supposed to occur behind that magic door. But it was during this course and those moments of quiet meditation that I often experienced my disease symptoms ceasing completely. It was nothing short of miraculous.

So, I started making space to practice mindfulness meditation daily. I'll point out here that I am not naturally a morning person at all. These days, I like to be at my desk in my home office by 10am. And by 10am, I mean noon. But at that time, I had a job that made me get up super early, and yet I would still set my alarm to get up a few minutes earlier just so I could drag myself into my yoga room at 7am and practice five minutes of meditation – it was THAT worth it.

Now, I know it's annoying when people say, *I bet you could find five minutes* – like you're not already packed to the gills. But...I bet you *could* find five minutes in your schedule, too. While this book is primarily about making changes on the inside, you'll discover that in order to make the space for those inside changes to occur, you might have to make a few tiny tweaks on the outside – like finding your own five minutes. But nothing too extreme, I promise.

But this isn't a book specifically about mindfulness meditation, it's a book about how to feel better, how to find that elusive sense of peace, ease, joy and balance, and how to awaken to the deeper levels of your life – your soul and your spirit. And there are so many paths we can take to get there. In this book, you'll encounter twelve other interesting practices that I hope will provide you with a similarly peaceful destination.

And keep in mind that peace, ease, joy and balance aren't really a "destination" at all – they are more of a way of experiencing life. A new way that replaces the old way of scarcity, struggle, and suffering. There's an idea that has been expressed by many wise folks across time – the idea that while life will necessarily include pain and difficulty, we do not actually have to suffer. The suffering part is up to us. It doesn't mean that we stop feeling the pain that is an inevitable part of life, or start doubling down on making everything perfect – in fact, it's just the opposite. We start feeling everything, even the hard parts, because feeling is what shakes us back alive. And we let go of the myth of perfection, and instead embrace becoming real.

A Medicinal Cocktail of Soul Healing Tools

For me, it wasn't just one thing that brought peace into my life – it was the alchemy of a few tools working in tandem. For example, around the same time that I started with the mindfulness meditation, I also hired a life coach. I wasn't actually looking for a life coach, I was looking for a business coach because I thought, *surely there isn't a better time to try to start a business than in the middle of my health falling apart?*

Good thing I hired a life coach that was willing to work on business stuff with me, and good thing we never actually got around to the business stuff. Surprisingly...there was plenty of life stuff to work on first. Hiring a life coach was a big decision and a large investment of time and money, but it was one of the best decisions I've made in my entire life.

But because I'm saving you time (and money) you don't have to run out and hire a life coach right now, you can just go ahead and continue reading this book! You're welcome. In all seriousness, though, there are parts of the journey where you might feel compelled to reach out for extra support. Whether that's in the form of a coach, therapist, doctor, healer, spiritual guide, trusted friend or anyone else, please do so. As I said in the note at the beginning of this book, there's no shame in the healing journey and you certainly don't need to feel like you have to do this all alone. However, this book is an excellent starting place. Here I've consolidated for you much of what I've learned over the years from my own experiences of being both client and coach.

For example, in addition to the mindfulness meditation and life coaching, I started keeping a Celebration/Gratitude Journal, prompted all those years ago by my amazing life coach, Michelle Stimpson. This practice also took me about five minutes because I used a very small journal so I couldn't overcomplicate the process (I'm going to assume I'm not the only recovering perfectionist here who knows how to overcomplicate absolutely anything). Five minutes in the morning for mindfulness meditation, and five minutes in the evening for my gratitude journal. We'll explore a gratitude practice in depth together later in this book, in Chapter 4, during the month of June. And I'll address all the reasons why you might not want to keep a gratitude journal so that the practice is super simple and feels truly *authentic*.

And lastly, during that time I also started practicing a lot of Yin yoga, which I found due to the intense Crohn's disease pain and inflammation restricting the style of yoga I could practice. Goodbye to my sweaty, acrobatic Ashtanga yoga; hello to a quietly powerful Yin yoga. While we won't explore the physical practice of Yin yoga together in this book, you'll find that one of the most important principles underlying everything in this book is the idea of rebalancing our "yin" energy.

For me, at that time, it was the cocktail of mindfulness meditation, gratitude journaling, and rebalancing my "yin" energy that became the medicine my soul desperately needed to feel better. By reading this book and playing around with the practices here, I hope you'll discover your own medicinal cocktail of soul healing tools.

A Word on Perfectionism

At this point, I consider myself a recovering perfectionist. The perfectionism used to be the driver in the car of my life, taking me for all kinds of chaotic rides. But now I see it for what it is, and I choose to drive my car myself. Sometimes it rears up and tries to take the wheel, wrapping its tentacles around me, but I'm much better about saying *hey, perfectionism, I see you and I hear you, but I'm going to drive this car myself, so please go sit down and take your freaky little tentacles off me.*

And I found that, while trying to break away from that old habit, anything that even hints at needing to show up with perfection doesn't feel good anymore. So, there's definitely no need for perfection here. Repeat to yourself: *there's no right way, only my way.* My own life coach ironed that mantra into my brain and it was a lifesaver.

If you, too, are showing up to this journey with some active habits like perfectionism or control, just use that to your advantage to help you get these new habits started. And then over time, I think you'll find that these new practices will help to soften out the hard edges of the old patterns and replace them with something even better: YOU driving your own car, peacefully and with ease.

In my past days as a Holistic Nutrition Coach, there was a similar principle that I loved to use with clients: *crowding out.* The idea was that instead of restricting yourself from being able to eat all the "bad" foods, you instead start introducing all of the "good" foods. And over time…the good foods start to crowd out the bad foods. It's a slower practice, but it requires less force and control in the short-term, and is more sustainable in the long-term. So, don't worry about the "bad" habits you might be bringing to the table right now; just get those new habits going and let them do their work of crowding out the old.

Make Sure it Feels Good to Your Soul

Long ago, before I realized that healing was much more of an inside job, I tried an endless array of things that I assumed were going to help me feel better in the long run, and I decided to do it all perfectly, but I forgot to pay attention to the most important thing: *how they were making me feel in the present moment.*

And if there's one thing I've learned through all of this, it's that you're not going to heal if you hate your healing plan

– no matter how much perfection you bring to the table. I learned that the hard way when I ended up in the hospital facing three serious intestinal surgeries despite following my nutritional "healing plan" perfectly – the healing plan that was stressing me out, flaring up my perfectionist all-or-none tendencies, and sucking the joy from my heart.

When I ended up in the hospital, I felt...*relief.* You don't need to end up in a hospital just to experience a moment of taking a breath, getting out of your own way, and stopping all the things you're doing that are actually stressing you out. I learned that lesson so that you don't have to!

But I am still very grateful that I tried all those things that were new to me at the time, because the ones that did have a positive impact had a hugely positive impact. Mindfulness, gratitude, and the general rebalancing of my "yin" energy aren't extremely complicated things – but it is actually insane to me how much these practices changed my outlook on life. I went through some of the worst and most trying times with my health and the Crohn's disease shortly after instituting these rituals – spending thirty-days in a hospital, a botched surgery that caused six-months of complications, and wasting away to a frail 100-pound skeleton – yet when I read back over my Gratitude Journal from those times, I'm like, *who is this wise person and why is she so calm?* Those practices were a lifesaver.

Now it's your turn. Go forth to meet and unleash the wise, calm, peaceful person that lives inside of YOU. Just make sure that whatever you choose to do feels right to you and doesn't become an added source of stress. If you try one of the ideas in this book and find it's not for you, let it go. Just give the practices a whirl and discover what feels good to your soul.

The Moral of the Story

So, what does this all come down to? Knowing where to start.

Being awake enough to say: *this is not the way I want to live my life.*

Being brave enough to realize: *it's not actually my job to carry the weight of the whole entire world on my two small shoulders and if I don't do something about it, it will in fact, crush me, and that will in fact, help no one.*

Being courageous enough to say: *I deserve to feel so much better!*

Close your eyes right now, and take a slow deep breath. Check in with your heart, check in with your mind, check in with your body, check in with your soulful inner knowing – and ask yourself, is there anything you would change if you could?

If you're waiting for some perfect moment in the future when life will be calm enough to bestow peace, ease, balance, and joy upon your life, I'm afraid you might never get there. Life's endless chaos will likely continue – just giving you all the more reason to seek peace and ease now.

I know it can feel like an insurmountable task to change patterns and behaviors that have been ingrained in you for years. It's work I continue on with even today, as I discover ever-deepening healing layers. But like my dad always used to remind me whenever I was feeling overwhelmed: *"How do you eat an elephant? One bite at a time."** Take that first bite, that first small step, and I promise you that peace and ease are just around the corner.

---

* *No elephants were harmed in the making of this book.*

A Journey of Inner Transformation

"Who looks outside, dreams; who looks inside, awakes."[1]

-Carl Jung

How to Use This Book

This is a self-coaching journey over the course of a year, organized by season – Spring, Summer, Late Summer, Fall and Winter. Each month, there's an essay with stories and teachings to offer inspiration as well as a deeper connection with the seasonal energy around us, followed by a practice to engage more deeply with the content. The months within each season are based on living in the Northern Hemisphere; if you live in the Southern Hemisphere, you can follow along with the same seasonal headings and markers of time, but just note that the months will be different for you.

You'll notice that this yearlong journey begins in March, and not in January as you might expect. The reason for this is because we are starting our journey in the season of spring, the "new year" of nature, rather than January, the calendar new year. You'll find the months of January and February towards the end of the book inside the "Winter" section! But honestly, it doesn't really matter what month you decide to start your journey in, because the cycle of the seasons is circular with no true "beginning" or "end." So, jump in wherever you are.

The idea is that you can either read the book all at once to get a feel for the whole cycle of the seasons, and then go back and focus in on the one singular practice associated with whatever month you're currently in; OR you can engage with it in a slow-drip fashion, savoring each chapter month-by-month as your trusty guide and companion for your journey of evolution throughout the year. It's kind of like having me in your pocket all year whispering helpful reminders to you throughout each month. Creepy, or super cool.

This is also a "do-less" approach. So, none of the practices are meant to be very time-consuming, and there's purposely only one practice per month so that you don't have to implement a whole bunch of new stuff all of once, which always feels overwhelming – and doesn't tend to stick.

Some of these practices may prompt you to want to make big changes to your life. While that may – in the end – be something you find yourself compelled and excited to do, it's not the main goal. Because sometimes it's not about changing your life; sometimes it's about changing the way you *experience* your life.

My shamanic teacher, Amy Wilinski, always reiterated an important teaching shared among many shamanic teachers:

"A shaman changes their world by changing their perception."[2] But the good news is – you're not required to be a shaman to do that. We all have the power to change our perception. And we can do it right now.

Most of the practices in this book call for changes in our internal worlds. I've found in my own life and experience that the most sustainable, and therefore impactful, changes happen in our lives not from the outside in – but from *the inside out.*

This is a book that I hope will shift your relationship to your inner world.

The Three Principles for Inside Out Change

How do we shift our relationship to our inner world? We start to integrate the following three principles:

1. **INNER BALANCE: We rebalance our yin and yang sides.**

Regardless of gender, we all have two sides - our divine feminine, or "yin" energy, and our sacred masculine, or "yang" energy. Our yin side has become overshadowed in our fast *go, go, go* and *do, do, do* culture, leading us to feel overworked, overwhelmed and burned out. This overshadowing is at the root of the deep imbalance we feel – individually and as a society.

2. **INNER ALIGNMENT: We realign with nature's cycles (and our own ebb and flow).**

In aligning with the outer forces of nature and the seasons, we create the ability to honor our own energetic ebb and flow: the natural phases we experience for growth and outward expansion, as well as the needed phases for rest and introspection.

3. **INNER CONNECTION: We reconnect with our intuition.**

Instead of feeling thrown about by the advice of every single voice out there, we learn to trust our own inner wisdom, the voice that keeps us connected to our highest self, and therefore always aligned with our highest path.

As you move through this book, you will find practices and inspirations that help you naturally engage with these three principles – inner balance though embracing your overshadowed yin side; inner alignment by honoring the seasonal cycles and your own personal ebb and flow; and inner connection via learning to trust your intuition – that allow you to practice the highest form of self-care: *soul-care.*

The Four Practices of Not-Doing

You'll also discover that self-care, or soul-care, doesn't have to be something that you *do* at all. In fact, it's more of a practice of removal. As the wise Taoist philosopher Lao Tzu has said, *"To attain knowledge, add things every day; to attain wisdom, remove things every day."*[3]

We can begin to remove things from our own lives everyday by practicing what I call the 4 S's: Slowness, Stillness, Silence, and Surrender.

1. **SLOWNESS: To embrace slowness, we remove constant doing.**

This is about removing our intrinsic need to *do, do, do;* our incessant drive to accomplish, achieve, and be endlessly productive. By the end of this book, I want you to feel that it's ok to do less – and to believe that it's actually necessary for your well-being!

2. **STILLNESS: To experience stillness, we remove constant going.**

This is about removing the need to *go, go, go*; our inability to be fully present in each moment, and our tendency to distract ourselves from our true self by never allowing ourselves to be at home. Our true home, the one that is always with us no matter where we physically are – is the home inside of ourselves. That is the home we truly need to see, to explore, to spend time with, and really get to know. By the end of this book, I want you to feel inspired to return to your true home!

3. **SILENCE: To experience silence, we remove constant noise.**

This includes the noise outside of ourselves that keeps us distracted from our true selves: the news, social media, TV, Netflix, even music when we habitually use it as a way to distract ourselves from something we don't want to feel. But also, the inside noise that bombards us – the constant flurry of thoughts inside our own minds that we cannot seem to escape, and the unnerving stream of emotions that live inside our bodies that we do not understand what to do with. By the end of this book, I want you to begin learning how to sit with true silence – not an oppressive and unnerving silence, but one that nourishes and heals.

4. **SURRENDER: And to embrace surrender, we remove control.**

This is about removing our attachment to a particular outcome or to things needing to be a particular way. The art of surrender can be physical – teaching us to surrender our physical body by becoming aware of the tension we hold, so that it can melt away to softness.

It can also be mental and emotional – teaching us to become more resilient to stress by surrendering our mind and heart to whatever is happening in that moment.

And it can be spiritual – when we allow ourselves to be open to a force greater than ourselves; where life moves from meaningless to meaningful. If we are so intent on things turning out our way on our timeline, holding on to our sense of control, we completely close ourselves off to the possibility of things turning out even better than we had hoped for, or simply taking a different path to get there. Surrender in this sense is trust, it is faith, it is openness, it is non-attachment – it is also delight and wonder and innocence and pure joy.

You can utilize my personal mantra of surrender that I turn to whenever things don't seem to be going exactly the way I would like them to: *everything is unfolding perfectly.* Just remember that it's not about your own version of perfect, this is about divine perfection. By the end of this book, I want you to understand that surrender doesn't mean giving up altogether; it means letting go of the often-stressful grip of control we cling to, and inviting in the possibility of wonder and greatness.

Enjoy the Slow Journey

Because this book is organized by month, after reading through the rest of the introduction, you might choose to jump ahead to the chapter that correlates with the current month that you're in now to begin your journey there. Or, you might choose to begin with March, where the book begins with the "new beginnings" energy of springtime, and read all the way through to get a feel for the entire cycle, paying extra attention to the practice that corelates to the month you're in now.

But the main thing to remember is – take it slowly! Don't feel that you have to rush. This is the journey of your life – allow yourself to go deep within and savor each practice. It's intentional that there's only one practice per month because I want this to feel do-able, and be sustainable. So, you can just focus on one practice, one month at a time.

You also don't have to do the practices at all, and can opt to simply read the book. It's your journey. The one thing I will advise regarding that though, is that the practices are designed to take whatever it is that you're learning about that month from the level of the mind into the deeper levels of the body, heart, soul and spirit – to transform the information provided from knowledge to wisdom. This is where the real transformation can take place, when we allow ourselves to really embody information, rather than simply knowing about it. Plus, the practices are fun.

Feel free to tweak the practices too, if you feel there's a way that would serve your purposes better, work more naturally for you, or generally feel more exciting to you. There's no right or wrong way, there's only your way.

However you choose to use this book, I wish you well on your journey!

PART I

SPRING

Spring Intro:
New Beginnings

SPRING! A TIME OF NEW BEGINNINGS, growth, outward expansion, abundance, beauty, the fullness of life. This is a season of *"new yang"* energy – meaning we are beginning the cycle of turning our attention outward, engaging with the world around us after the long dark of winter and our time of introspection, rest, reflection. The world around us wakes up after her long slumber, and we, too, feel ourselves excited to once again *go, go, go*, and *do, do, do!*

I decided to start our journey of soul-healing and spirit-dancing here because this is a place we are already quite familiar and comfortable with: *doing, doing, doing*, and *going, going, going*, often in a nonstop circle to burnout. But, this year, we're committed to doing things differently!

To avoid the eventual crash and burnout, this year we'll pay a little more attention to our yin side. While we want to honor the sacredness of new beginnings, this year we'll do so in a way that is less about external markers of success and achievement, and more about what makes you feel good in your soul.

In March, at the very beginning of the unfolding spring season, before it even looks like spring around us, we'll set intentions – plant some dream seedlings for the future – that are aligned with your innermost feelings and desires, that help usher us into our next becoming as we awaken at that deeper level, the level of the soul.

Then in April, aligned with those cleansing spring rains around us, we'll release the old conditioning, behaviors, and limiting beliefs that are sapping our time and energy, so you can clear the decks for something new – and better – to emerge.

And to keep us aligned with our innermost selves throughout the year, in May, at the time of spring's fullest abundance, we'll start really honing our ability to listen to – *and trust* – our intuition, that inner compass that will keep you soul-aligned and spirit-dancing through your own abundance all year long.

May you enjoy the journey and practices of spring as you prepare to usher in your own new beginnings!

CHAPTER 1

March:
Planting Seeds

"YOU ARE HERE TO LIVE IN JOY, *everything else is extra,"* Celtic shamanic teacher and healer Amantha Murphy said at a recent training I attended. She went on to explain: *"You don't have to go out and make your mark, that is your only job: being at ease, in joy. Then you gift that opportunity to others simply by your being."*[4]

What a concept, right? We tend to think our purpose here is to make money, or make children, or make a name for ourselves, or change the world in big systemic ways. But do we consider that it might be our purpose to be JOYFUL? How drastically would we have to alter our lives and our jobs and our aspirations if every day our main goal was to be *joyful?* How many of us truly feel joyful on most days? With the way the world has been the last couple years during the Covid pandemic, how many of us are just hoping for feeling OK?

I think the reason that true joy can feel so out of reach is that so many of us live our lives out of alignment with the desires of our soul. And we instead create a life based on the "*shoulds*." And based on the expectations layered upon us by family, society, our jobs, our roles. Until we're a body and a life filled with "*shoulds*" instead of filled with SOUL.

But how do we make such a drastic change?

A Closing Door, A New Beginning

Around the time I was writing this essay, I did something I often do as part of my morning meditation practice: consult some oracle cards. For those who are new to them, oracle cards are a fun and tangible tool for practicing getting in touch with your intuition, that deep inner wisdom that lives inside each of us. You'll learn how to conduct your own oracle card practice in Chapter 11 during the month of January, or you can flip ahead to that part early if you're feeling called to that.

The first card I pulled was from a beautiful deck called *The Shaman's Dream Oracle* by Alberto Villoldo & Collete Baron-Reid. The card was called the "*Closing Door*" and its message was about recognizing what is ending in your life, as well as seeing the positive aspects of endings – as opportunities to create the space to call in your greater purpose.[5]

Then I pulled a second card from a different deck, one that is so deeply tied to the wisdom of the natural world around us, called *Sacred Destiny Oracle: A 52 Card Deck to Discover the Landscape of Your Soul* by Denise Linn. The card was called "*New Beginnings: Radiant Sunrise*" and its message was about moving from the darkness into the light, beginning a new cycle, as well as expansion, new experiences, opportunities, and the birth of new ideas.[6]

It was after pulling the second card that I realized how perfect these messages were for right now. A closing door and a new beginning? What signifies that more than the seasonal shift of winter into spring, a whole new cycle of life beginning again as we move into the light and leave behind us the dark of winter.

How even more significant at this moment in time as we take a deep breath after the last few years of the pandemic. The pandemic did give us a gift – those years were an *advanced initiation* into our lives, giving us an opportunity for an awakened sense of deeper meaning and greater purpose. We stand now upon a new threshold – after the initiation, the emergence. After the winter, the spring. After the closing door, a new beginning.

We now have the opportunity to close the door on what we know isn't right for us, to shed some of these heavy expectations and "*shoulds*" that have been the foundation of our lives for so long – as well as an opportunity to take a step towards what is right for us, towards what speaks to our soul and fills us with joy. As Amantha told us, "*You are here to live in joy, everything else is extra.*" Life is too short, and also too long, to be living in a way that doesn't make your soul happy. Remember this.

The times that force us to turn inward, introspect, and question our life choices gift us with an immense pool of data about ourselves from which we can choose to learn and make these conscious shifts. We can embrace this element that came out of the hopefully once-in-a-lifetime global pandemic of 2020-23 – as well as the times like the much less dramatic yearly season of winter itself.

But it's also easy to allow ourselves to slip back into a mindless unconsciousness of routine. The pull back into comfortability and our narrow band of what is safe and known can be strong. Stay awake! Stay conscious. You deserve to be joyful.

A Future We Want to Visit

In 2018, the following message from renowned theoretical physicist and cosmologist Stephen Hawking was beamed into space by Hawking's family and the European Space Agency. It's destination? The nearest black hole that it should reach in about 3,500 years:

> *"One of the great revelations of the Space Age has been the perspective it has given humanity on ourselves. When we see the earth from space, we see ourselves as a whole. We see the unity and not the divisions. It is such a simple image with a compelling message. One planet. One human race.*
>
> *We are here together and we need to live together with tolerance and respect. We must become Global Citizens. Our only boundaries are the way we see ourselves. The only borders, the way we see each other.*
>
> *We are all time travelers, journeying together into the future. But let us work together to make that future a place we want to visit. Be brave, be determined, overcome the odds. It can be done."[7]*

This message is a good reminder to stop and zoom out of the typically zoomed in perspective of our lives. To remember that we're more than just the trees we can see around us – we're part of an entire forest, an entire ecosystem of human beings surrounding the globe. All of us looking up at the same sky, all of us with our feet planted upon the same

Planet Earth. But let us hope that it takes us a good deal less than 3,500 years to heed this message and reach *our* destination: *a future we want to visit.*

We've created so many distinctions between ourselves, polarized ourselves into so many competing camps, because we forget that we are more alike than we are different. But we can only meet each other as deeply as we've met ourselves. We can only truly understand and appreciate another human being when we can truly understand and appreciate ourselves. We can only accept the darkness and the flaws and the faults in another when we can accept the darkness and flaws and faults in ourselves. And we can only truly encourage another human being to shine their light brightly when we've given ourselves permission to shine our own.

When we haven't encountered the faults inside of ourselves and learned to grow through them and love ourselves because of them, we judge others for their shortcomings. When we haven't discovered the unique gifts inside of ourselves that only we can bring to this world and given ourselves permission to shine brightly, we yearn for or envy the success of others.

It is both our darkness AND our light that we tend to be most blind to, and so we keep ourselves living inside a narrow zone of comfortability and safety. As Hawking observed, we create boundaries in the way we see ourselves, borders in the way we see others. And bound by our judgments and yearnings and envy, we create for ourselves a comfortable prison. But life is meant to be a playground. Yes, we get scraped and bruised on the playground, we fall down and get back up, we play and fight and make up, we find our tribe, get kicked out of our tribe, and find a new tribe all on the playground. But underneath all of this, weaving it all together, what do we always find on a playground? Joy.

The Gift of Free Will

I had an interesting convo with a friend recently about free will and pre-determination. She expressed hating the trope that *"everything happens for a reason,"* as it seems to presume that every single thing is predetermined, as though we have no choices that we can make for ourselves. What about free will?? I agree that free will is vitally important! I also believe that life gets most exciting when we weave the concepts of predetermination and free will *together*.

The reason I believe that free will does exist is because if everything was exclusively pre-determined by a benevolent force, I think we would all be lovely angelic beings. We would be living in Paradise. It is precisely because we have free will that we have been able to make such unhappy choices for our planet, for the way we treat each other, and perhaps in our own lives. That's the "gift" of free will.

But the gift of free will also means that at any given moment we can choose to take a different action than what we've taken before. And every action we take cumulatively adds up, in our own lives as well as together as a global society. Free will is our gift, as well as our responsibility.

While I believe that learning to surrender our tight grip of control is a vital aspect of healing and a pathway to allowing peace, ease and joy to enter our lives, we also must remember the role we play in our own lives. I think it benefits us to see life as a co-creation between ourselves and a force greater than our own flesh and bones, where we can see ourselves as both artist *and* divinely created masterpiece. Both created, and creator. That is true empowerment.

If it is because of free will and our ability to make our own choices that we don't live in Paradise, I would argue that it is that very same free will and our ability to make our own choices that can take us there. What actions do you want to be contributing to your own life? To the collective? Are you contributing to keeping things the same? Or contributing to a different kind of future? Spring is about new beginnings. What will you choose to begin anew? How will you fulfill your purpose to live joyfully in alignment with the desires of your soul?

As Hawking advised, *"We are all time travelers, journeying together into the future. But let us work together to make that future a place we want to visit."* So, here's to creating a future you want to visit! May you heed the call of your soul, have the courage to recognize what is no longer serving you, and find JOY in new beginnings this spring.

-MARCH PRACTICE-

INNER GARDENING: THE ART OF BECOMING

During this winter into spring transition time, spend some time pondering the reflection questions that follow and doing a little of your own "Inner Gardening." Plant some intentions and dream seedlings for the future, that are aligned with your innermost feelings and desires, and begin to awaken at the deeper level of the soul.

Honoring the Inner Work Beneath the Surface

When a plant grows into its full potential, we get to benefit from the external manifestation of this: the beauty that it brings to our lives. But we rarely think about all the inner work that the plant had to go through in order to bring us it's hallmark spring color. The fully formed flower doesn't just pop up in late spring saying, *"Hello! I am suddenly here out of nowhere!"* That's what we see, but we know that a lot occurs behind the scenes before we are graced with that chapter.

And that's the work that's occurring now, around us in nature, and within us as well. In the earliest moments of spring, before we see any external results whatsoever, while we feel discouraged at how long it's taking for spring to truly arrive, so much inner work is occurring just beneath the surface of nature. And this is the time to honor the inner work that occurs inside of YOU just beneath the surface, as well!

3 Steps to Inner Gardening:

1. Enjoy some quiet reflection time to connect with your inner soul self, as described in Step 1 below.

2. Immediately follow that with the journaling/planning questions listed in Step 2. You might discover that it's easier to answer those questions once you've shifted yourself into the parasympathetic mode where you can more easily tap into your intuition, or your deep inner knowing. And you make that shift through the act of slowing down and breathing deeply.

3. Then use the springtime mantras listed in Step 3 to stay peacefully inspired throughout the season!

Step 1: Connect with Your Inner Self

The first practice that I recommend to master the art of Inner Gardening is to sit quietly for a few minutes in contemplation. This could be seated, lying down, or in a chair curled up in the sun, indoors or out, whatever feels best to you. Close your eyes, begin to breathe slowly and deeply, and present to yourself the following questions:

Who am I when I'm not doing?

Who am I when I'm not thinking?

These questions may feel foreign or confusing at first; they could provoke some anxiety or restlessness. But don't feel pressure to "figure it out" with your mind. This is not a journaling exercise (unless you later feel called to jot down some insights about it). You don't need to produce an answer at all. The idea here is not to wrestle with these questions with your mind, but to simply sit with the questions as you breathe.

This begins to orient us to the deeper layers of who we are, beyond the level of the body and the mind. It reminds us that beyond all our many external actions of going and doing and cultivating our outer worlds, we also have a heart that beats with desire and passion, that speaks to us as the voice of the soul – *if we know how to listen.* It also reminds us that we have a soul that wants nothing more than to reach its potential, to grow into its highest purpose in this life, to be explored deeply with all its wounds and its darkness, and lovingly guided to heal; to be honored for its many gifts and shining brightness, to be reintegrated back into the fabric of our body and mind.

This heart and soul is also you. Sometimes, we just forget. So, it's time to get reacquainted. I've heard it said that while prayer is considered *speaking* to God/Goddess/Universe/ The Divine/our Higher Self, meditation is the act of *listening.* So, close your eyes and listen deeply: *Who am I when I'm not doing? Who am I when I'm not thinking?*

Set a timer so you can just let go and not have to worry about how long it's been. If you're new to any kind of formal meditation practice, start with five minutes.

Step 2: Plan Your Garden

This is the part of the practice where I do recommend you get out a journal or notebook. After you've spent some time breathing slowly and deeply, and sitting with the above contemplation questions, then open up to a fresh page in your journal, divide it into four sections, and write one of these questions at the top of each section (or if you know you like to write a lot, use a fresh page for each question):

1. *What do I wish to grow more of in my life?*

2. *What do I need to let go of in order to create the SPACE for this?*

3. *What wisdom am I bringing with me from the dark of winter?*

4. *Who am I becoming? What am I awakening within myself?*

Then, decide how much time you'd like to spend reflecting on each question. If your time is limited or you find journaling annoying, you might set a timer for 10 minutes for the whole exercise. If you have a lot of time and love this kind of thing, give yourself 10 minutes per question. Whatever feels right.

If you dislike the idea of journaling, but love the idea of planning – remind yourself that this is a planning exercise at its heart! We're planning out our inner garden. Sometimes I love to journal and other times "journaling" can sound like a task to me, depending on how I'm feeling. But planning, oh I always love to plan! Whatever you need to do to get yourself excited about the prospect. Change your world by changing your perspective.

Here are some helpful notes to get you started pondering each question:

GUIDANCE FOR QUESTION 1 –

The energy of spring is all about AWAKENING. It is a time of growth and rebirth. Starting fresh, beginning anew. While I'm sure you're quite familiar with the idea of planning out a garden in your yard, have you ever stopped to consciously plan out your inner garden?

The first and most important step in planning out any garden is to ask yourself, what am I actually planning to grow? The same is true for your inner garden: *what do I wish to grow more of in my life?*

Remember that this could be something external and tangible like a new house or a new job, but it could also be something internal and intangible – like peace and ease, balance, free time, white space on your calendar, fun, joy, compassion, gratitude, or a stronger connection to your intuition or inner child.

This isn't about what you think you "should" grow more of in your life. "Shoulds" don't make your soul sing. What makes you feel excited, joyful or peaceful when you think about it? Ponder, and then answer this question in your notebook. *What do I wish to grow more of in my life?*

GUIDANCE FOR QUESTION 2 –

The second step in yard gardening is the logistical one that comes down to a matter of space. If we try to cram too much into our garden, it threatens the survival of any one plant in the garden, so we might have to make some cuts – *to allow the space for growth to occur.*

In addition to scaling back our plan in order to leave space for growth, we also need to do the important step of removing the old. Pulling out the old, dead roots in order to create a fresh canvas for new beginnings.

The same is true again for our inner garden – after getting clear on what it is we hope and intend to cultivate in our lives and in ourselves, we must also ask ourselves, *what do I need to let go of in order to create the space for this?*

Here's where I want to challenge you. We are so accustomed to looking at our outer lives and making the assessment that this is the entirety of who we are; but the act of inner gardening occurs on the inside. So, what can you let go of from your inner world?

And though these changes are occurring on the inside, Inner Gardening absolutely can have an external result or manifestation – think about growing more love in your life by letting go of harshly judging yourself; the result might be not only an improved relationship with yourself, but deeper, more loving and truly understanding connections with everyone around you as well. Inner change, outer result.

So, consider your letting go on a few levels:

- The tangible level if you've got too much stuff crammed into your calendar and to-do lists.
- The physical level if you're needing to find a way to let go of tension, pain, and stress in the body.
- The mental level by letting go of limiting beliefs, negative spirals of thought, or untruths about yourself and your worth.
- The emotional level by letting go of heavy feelings, stuck emotions, or past hurts and resentments.
- The spiritual level by letting go of old and repeating patterns, as well as healing past triggers and wounds.

After the dark there is awakening, there is a welcoming of the new. But before the new can arrive, there must be a letting go, a clearing out of the old. And as Lao Tzu wisely reminds us: *"When I let go of what I am, I become what I might be."*[8] Remember there are no right or wrong answers here;

jot down whatever feels right to you in this moment. *What do I need to let go of in order to create the SPACE for this?*

GUIDANCE FOR QUESTION 3 –

I want to give an extra nod to this question: *What wisdom am I bringing with me from the dark of winter?* It's always an important question to ponder in any year as we transition from winter into spring, but we can also take a wider view of this question, as well. We have just spent not only the past winter, but the past few years of the Covid pandemic living through a time that a teacher of mine referred to as *"shining light in dark places."* For many of us, the pandemic was its own brand of darkness. Maybe you've taken advantage of the last few years to do some inner reflecting. If not, do some now. What shadowy corners and long forgotten dark places within you have been illuminated by the energy of the past few years?

We tend to stow away in our inner shadows not only the painful parts of ourselves that we'd like to pretend didn't exist, but also the brilliant parts we've simply forgotten. Discovering both has immense powers for healing.

Reflect on this past winter season, the last few years, or both, and then jot down some notes about it. *What wisdom am I bringing with me from the dark of winter?*

GUIDANCE FOR QUESTION 4 –

This last set of questions is perhaps my favorite: *Who am I becoming? What am I awakening within myself?* It reminds us to redirect our focus back to our inner world, back to who we *are* versus what we *do.*

Getting to know who we are on the inside is one of the most important steps we can take towards our personal development, our soul growth, and our healing work that returns us to our lost sense of wholeness.

Spring is an amazing time to do this work. Just be careful of the trap of busyness and distraction! Spring and then summer arrive, and we sometimes find it such a welcome change from the slow and quiet of winter that we accidentally get so caught up in doing and going and distracting ourselves that we lose this opportunity to really AWAKEN at a deeper level, *the level of the soul.*

So, take a moment to reflect on these questions, and then record some thoughts and feelings about it in your notebook. *Who am I becoming? What am I awakening within myself?*

Step 3: Choose Your Way

The third practice I recommend in your Inner Gardening adventure is to write down the following sayings, put them somewhere where you will see them, and return to them every time you start to feel anxious that things aren't progressing fast enough in your life, or the external result you're expecting isn't arriving on the schedule you had hoped for.

Return to them every time you start to get down on yourself for not "accomplishing" enough today, every time you notice yourself getting swept up in busyness and distraction and an outer world focus that is disconnected from your inner world heart and soul:

"SITTING QUIETLY, DOING NOTHING, SPRING COMES AND THE GRASS GROWS BY ITSELF."
-ZEN SAYING BY MATSUO BASHO[9]

"NATURE DOES NOT HURRY, YET EVERYTHING IS ACCOMPLISHED."
-LAO TZU[10]

These sayings help to remind us that there is a balance needed between going out into the world and *making things happen* – and allowing things to happen as they are meant to happen according to divine timing and a grander plan. We can find that balance by seeing ourselves as both sacred creator via our free will, as well as the divinely created masterpiece.

They remind us that beyond the way we have been trained to believe is the only way – the way of force and action – there is a second way: the way of receptivity and flow. You can be the salmon fighting to swim upstream – and sometimes this is the appropriate course of action – or you can be the river itself, eternally flowing on your perfect path. Since you are neither a salmon nor a river, you get to choose. What happens if you let go just a bit and surrender to the flow of your own divine path?

Remember to keep returning to these sayings to stay peacefully inspired throughout the whole spring season, or anytime you need those reminders. Happy Inner Gardening! May you enjoy this opportunity to plant some seeds of joy and truly awaken, at the deeper level of the soul.

CHAPTER 2

April:
Spring Cleaning

WHILE WINTER HAS BEEN our time for deep rest, restoration, quiet, healing, solitude, and stillness...spring is our time for *growth*. This is the time when Mother Nature begins to awaken from her deep slumber, to create the earliest rumblings of growth deep below the surface, to begin the trajectory towards the full manifestation and abundance of the summer. So, what does that mean for us as human beings? The same! We, too, start to awaken from the quiet of winter and we begin our own trajectory towards the abundance of life we experience in the summer.

Have you noticed the pace of your life getting a little more hectic lately? Projects and commitments coming out of the woodwork? It's those spring rumblings beginning! We feel our potential rising up inside of us, which we often experience as a pull to do more, go more, and sometimes even as uncomfortable feelings like anxiety, impatience or agitation.

Though January 1st may claim the title of New Year, it is spring that really marks the beginning of Nature's New Year. So, this is an excellent time for planting those seeds: setting intentions with the practice from last month and dreaming your big dreams for the future. It's a good time to know what you really want. And instead of doing this in the dead of winter when the calendar's new year rolls around – when we're in an energetic ebb – this is a time of year that naturally aligns us with the flow of energy within and around us.

So, with the right energetic conditions in place externally, let's continue tending to your inner conditions. And to aid us in this endeavor, this month we're going to take a deeper look at the Law of Attraction – on an energetic level that goes beyond the more surface aspects of positive thinking that can quickly border on toxic positivity or not feeling our real feelings, and beyond simply asking for money to suddenly appear in the mail – so that maybe this year we'll finally get what we really want. Or...perhaps instead of getting what we really want, we just might get what we *need*.

You Just Have to Want It...Right?!

The Law of Attraction is one of a handful of spiritual laws meant to explain the energetic nature of the universe, and the one that tends to get the most attention. There's a common saying regarding the Law of Attraction, have you heard it?

Whatever we think or feel, the universe says yes.

It always makes me think of this hilarious Saturday Night Live episode from way back in 2008 where Tina Fey and Amy Poehler address the nation as Sarah Palin while she's campaigning as McCain's running mate, and Hillary Clinton right after losing the Democratic party nomination to Obama. After Fey (as Palin) points out just how close she is to the White House, she says: *"It just goes to show that anyone can be President, all you have to do is WANT it."*

At which point Poehler (as Hillary) begins maniacally laughing while trying to maintain a professional face and says, *"YEAH, you know Sarah, looking back if I could change one thing, I probably should have WANTED it more."* And then resumes maniacally laughing while ragefully ripping off the side of the podium.[11]

It still makes me laugh so hard. Because we've all been there, right?! Those times when we've really wanted something and put all of our efforts and energy into that thing, and so according to the Law of Attraction, it should then happen...right?

But sometimes, it just doesn't. No matter how much we visualize it and think positively about it. No matter how badly we really do WANT it. So, what's going on then?

Brick by Brick: Makin' it Happen

When it comes to planting seeds, planning our destiny, and going after what we want, there is one very common way that we tend to go about this: free will and solo-creation. This is the path that we create, the one we lay down brick-by-brick, alone of our own volition using our own free will.

This is not typically known as the path of least resistance, but it is the one in which we continue to feel that we have the most control. This is the path we are often on when we are tapped only into our masculine side, our yang energy, our rational left brain.

There's a story I once heard about an individual who had a near-death experience and temporarily went to the other side. They met a guide there who showed them around, and at one point they saw a group of souls who were laying down bricks to create a path. This individual asked who they were and the guide explained that those are the *'free-willers.'* Since the guides aren't allowed to intervene from the other side unless asked, those individuals were laying down their own path brick by brick.

What an interesting image, right? Sometimes life does feel that way, doesn't it? That we're laying down our own paths brick by heavy brick by heavy brick. It's the price we pay to feel fully in control of our own destiny. But what if there was another way of going after what we want that didn't feel quite so heavy as though it were ours alone to shoulder?

For most of us, we only know some version of this first path, the one of pure free will, of *efforting*, of feeling that we alone must hold all the pieces together so that everything doesn't come crashing down. Our society is so overly tapped into our masculine/yang/ rational left-brain energy that it's the only path that tends to be modeled for us as a viable option. And it can be a rather exhausting place to be! I definitely know that firsthand, as I lived most of my life that way until my body finally broke down and forced me to find another way.

So, let's take a deeper look at this Law of Attraction, as this comes into play when we're on the second path, the path that we don't have to shoulder all alone, the path of receptivity and co-creation.

Aligning with the Weave: Co-Creating

The second way is the path that we allow to unfold, the one we co-create with assistance from the universe. This often *does* feel like the path of least resistance, although it is not entirely without blocks on the path that may be there to serve as course corrections or opportunities to lean in and grow. It is the path where we feel that we are in alignment with some magic of the universe, some moment of divine timing where the right people, places, things, and opportunities seem to find their way *to* us.

This is the path we are often on when we are additionally tapped into our feminine side, our yin energy, our intuitive right-brain. But this isn't about being *only* tapped into our feminine, yin, intuitive right-brain energy – we do want to be tapped into a healthy dose of our masculine, yang, rational left-brain energy also. To be a balanced human being, we need our ability to receive, as well as our ability to create.

It's just that most of us in our culture are tapped way too far into the masculine side – regardless of gender, as these are energies we all embody. So, the emphasis for a while is going to have to be on re-integrating the missing feminine half.

Instead of being in hunting mode only, going out and taking what is ours, we are allowing ourselves to sit back, tune in, and like a powerful magnet to attract and receive the right opportunities by allowing them to find their way *to* us. But this requires a degree of trust, patience, and a bit of inner work in advance!

Like a Song Stuck on Repeat: Ego Agenda vs. Soul Program

I think the way that we've come to think about and use the spiritual principle of the Law of Attraction is a little too...human. It's like we're still stuck in that first story, the one about free will and control, and then we just plastered the Law of Attraction on top of that, giving ourselves an even deeper sense of false personal control that we now have a tool to manifest whatever we want.

But the Law of Attraction is sneaky. Remember that saying, *whatever we think or feel, the universe says yes?* Remember how we decided it must be nonsense because this doesn't always happen no matter how badly we WANT something, and visualize it, and think positively about it?

Well guess what? The saying is actually true. We just don't know ourselves as well as we think we do. And we forget to consider an important aspect of our multi-faceted selves: our energetic body, or our Soul.

While we're busy writing down what we want in the physical realm, thinking positively about it in the mental realm, feeling only happy feels about it in the emotional realm...*the energetic realm?* It's sitting there as a massive holding pool of everything we no longer want, secretly and unintentionally sabotaging our best laid plans. Unless we attend to it. Which most of us don't.

As scholar and dream teacher Robert Moss says in one of his many fascinating books, *The Three Only Things: Tapping the Power of Dreams, Coincidence & Imagination:*

> *"Check on the personal history you may still be carrying in your energy field. You can defeat your own goals if you are freighted with the burdens of past shame and pain and failure so that your body does not believe you.*

The traditional Hawaiian healers known as kahunas have a profound teaching about this. They say that the ordinary mind has very little to do with creative manifestation. The best that can manifest in our lives comes through the creative partnership of the dense energy body (which they call the unihipilli) and the Higher Self (or aumakua). Get them working and playing together, and the ego will come along."[12]

So, what does that really mean? We typically try to manifest what we want in our lives from our *'small s'* ego self, as opposed to our *'capital S'* Higher Self. Or, from our *"ordinary mind"* as Moss puts it. But our old history stuck in our energy body gets in the way.

Our energy body stores the old stories, the old patterns, the old programming; the limiting beliefs from ourselves, our families, our society; the past hurts, shame, failures and losses; the repressed anger, frustrations and resentments. And unless we clear that out, we will continue to get more of the same in our lives. Like a song stuck on repeat.

Because guess what? The universe doesn't say yes to the desires of our ego or ordinary mind; it says yes to the stories of the energy body, to the program written into our soul. Whatever is written into your energy body or soul, is what you are unwittingly manifesting into your life. It's frustrating to consider that WE may be the ones preventing whatever it is we desperately want from showing up in our lives. But knowing this, we have the opportunity to do something about it.

The How-To

The key then to manifesting into our lives what it is we truly want and to stop inadvertently manifesting what we don't?

1. Clear out the old patterns, the old programming still living within you by deeply clearing out your energy body or Soul. You can use this month's Full Moon Releasing Ritual that follows as a starting point for this.

2. Align your intentions for the future not with the wants of the ordinary mind, but with the deepest desires of your Soul. Revisit what you wrote down in last month's practice of Inner Gardening when you consciously started planning out, *what do I wish to grow more of in my life?* How does that feel when you re-read what you wrote? Is there anything you feel called to tweak, add, or remove?

If you haven't done that practice in your journey yet, that's ok! You could take a moment now to reflect on that question (flip back to the practice from last month for some helpful tips) or just come back around to it next March on your next journey around the wheel.

3. Remember that once you enter into a co-creative partnership with the universe, it becomes less about what you want to manifest in a heavy brick-by-brick way, and more about being receptive, open, and curious to the opportunities you need that will soon be coming your way. It's about starting to release some of your own personal grip of control by sharing that burden with the universe.

We love to feel in control, but honestly, we're just giving ourselves too much human credit, and stressing ourselves out in the process! Instead, we can free up more space inside of ourselves to *play* on our path, and feel *peaceful* while doing so.

The Great Weave

Amantha Murphy says in her book, *The Way of the Seabhean: An Irish Shamanic Path:* "*Each one of us...creates our own unique weave which vibrates around us. This energetic weave attracts everything we need in life.*"[13]

But while we're getting busy with this inner work of cleaning up our side of the street and creating our unique web of attraction around ourselves, let us also remember our role in the grander scheme of things. As Amantha also says: "*The world is a weave of energy and every human being is a thread on that Great Weave.*"[14]

So, if we've done our inner work, and yet something still isn't coming to us in the way that we envisioned, or on the time schedule that we hoped for, it is helpful to remember we are all sacred weavers weaving our individual destinies together into one great tapestry. We may not receive what we WANT because what we *need* will allow us to weave an even brighter, more impactful thread into the tapestry of life.

And if you need a little inspiration for how you'll go about your new method for spring manifesting this year, you can always think of the master weaver, the Spider. Spider doesn't go out and expel all its energy hunting down what it wants; it joyfully and thoughtfully creates a web, and then it patiently waits on that web for the universe to bring it its lunch.

Disturbingly genius.

-APRIL PRACTICE-

FULL MOON RELEASING RITUAL

A Full Moon is energetically the perfect time for releasing! This month, align with the powerful feminine energy of the moon for an even deeper inner spring cleaning.

Since the date of the Full Moon changes every month, do a quick online search for "April full moon" for whatever year it is for you now to get the specific date. It's best if you can do this within a day or two of the Full Moon when the energy is the strongest. While anytime is a great time for releasing and letting go, it can feel even more powerful when done in alignment with the energy of the moon.

Performing a Full Moon Ritual:

1. CREATE A SACRED SPACE TO SIT AND BE PEACEFUL. You could go outside and do this sitting under the full moon, or sit indoors and light a candle, or whatever else feels right to you. Close your eyes and take a few slow deep breaths in and out of the nose to center yourself.

2. CLEANSE YOUR ENERGY AND YOUR SPACE. You might choose to light some incense or burn some cleansing herbs, or simply visualize a bright

golden light washing over you and cleansing your body, mind, heart and soul of all heavy energy.

3. **WRITE DOWN WHAT YOU INTEND TO RELEASE.** A Full Moon Ritual is about purging the heavy energies, limiting beliefs, and old habits that no longer serve you, the things you no longer wish for or need in your life, or anything you might have outgrown. Write down on a piece of paper what you choose to release: energies/habits/beliefs/people/places/things, etc. You could use this as an opportunity to name any unhealthy elements of doing, going, noise and attachment to control (see the 4 Practices of Not-Doing from the Introduction) that you're ready to release in the name of soul-care, as well! If you need some additional inspiration on what to release, go back to last month's Inner Gardening practice if you've already completed that, and see what you wrote down in response to the second question, *what do I need to release to create the space for this?* You might have your answer right there!

4. **BURN WHAT YOU'VE WRITTEN DOWN.** This is the fun part! As you burn your paper – either outdoors in your firepit, indoors in your fireplace, or over a fireproof dish – breathe deeply into your heart while you imagine and FEEL all of those things you wrote down leaving your life as they are carried away into the ethers. Say aloud or to yourself: *"I now release (fill in the blank), and so it is."*

5. **TAKE YOUR CLEANSING BREATHS.** Take ten deep breaths in through the nose and out through the mouth. Do this sitting or lying down. Make each exhale powerful, like a great sigh, or a big "whoosh" noise. With each exhale feel and imagine everything on the list you just burned leaving your body/mind/heart/soul/spirit.

6. **FINISH WITH THE FULL MOON RELEASING RITUAL AFFIRMATION STATEMENT.** See below! Say this out loud or to yourself to seal the practice.

Full Moon Releasing Ritual - Affirmation Statement:

I now release what no longer serves me.

I let it go from my heart, from my thoughts, from my soul, from my body, and from my spirit.

I remember that my biggest challenges are my greatest teachers, and I choose to let go any heaviness or negativity surrounding what I am releasing. I choose to thank this person or situation for teaching me a lesson I needed to experience in order for my soul to evolve.

I choose instead to create the space for that which does serve me: for joy, for abundance, for new possibilities that maybe right now I can't even predict.

But I am allowing myself to be open and ready by signaling to the Universe/God/Higher Power/Divine Energy that I have done my part through this personal inner clearing.

By letting go I create space, and I choose to fill this space with gratitude for the things in my life that do serve me –

the people/places/things/energies/beliefs/habits that support me on my journey to becoming the truest, most authentic manifestation of ME.

Going Forward

Remember that you can return to this practice every time there is a full moon, which means that every month you have an opportunity for some energetic cleansing. You'll also encounter a few other cleansing and releasing practices in Chapter 9 during the month of November. Some of those practices will get at even deeper layers of letting go and will make a great compliment to this monthly moon practice. You don't have to do this every month, just know that the option is there, and you can come back to it anytime you start to feel heavy and bogged down instead of spacious and light.

Each time you come to it, you may find that you have something new to release, or you may find that you're continuing to work on releasing elements of the same thing. Trust your intuition that there's no way you can do this wrong, and every time you come to this practice, you're helping to create the space inside of yourself to align with the good that is waiting to come to you.

Happy spring cleaning and spring manifesting! Here's to a whole new kind of spring cleaning – scouring your energetic slate clean. May you joyfully enter into a co-creation with the universe, weave your beautiful web, and receive everything you need for your soul to grow this spring.

May:
Inner Abundance

WELCOME TO LATE SPRING, where nature has fully awakened and winter is a distant memory! As we look around, we see Mother Nature has much to share with us as she's suddenly blossomed into her grandest show. And as we know by now, whatever is going on around us in nature speaks to what is occurring within us as well. And late spring is the season of…ABUNDANCE.

This is the time of full manifestation – happening around us, as well as within our own lives, based on what we began earlier in the season or year. Maybe you set some intentions with the New Year way back in January, or maybe you planted some dream seedlings via your Inner Gardening practice in Chapter 1 during the month of March – and you're now seeing those seeds beginning to sprout and take form.

Or maybe you didn't set any intentions or plant any seeds, and that's feeling startlingly clear now, too! In this chapter we'll be exploring how to truly feel the joyful abundance of your own life. Because sometimes, it just doesn't quite feel that way, does it?

The true essence of our own lives becomes a bit clearer and more evident in this season of abundance. What is it that we are actually growing in our own lives? What are we creating an abundance of? Flowers, or *weeds*? Joy, or *dissatisfaction*?

What's going on when the world is awash in springtime abundance, but you're just not feeling it in your own life? It might be a reality check about how you're living your life, and how out-of-alignment you might be with the messages of your soul.

Aligning with our Trusty Inner Compass

To truly bask in abundance, joy, and a feeling of manifesting our true purpose, we have to live in alignment with our soul. Otherwise, we are forever just left or right of center, forever longing for some feeling of completeness, wholeness, fullness that remains just out of reach. Forever rushing forward, but going...*where?* And why? For what?

So how do we stay aligned with our soul? We use our trusty inner compass – our intuition. When we're following our intuition, we are always on the path of our soul. No matter what is happening in our lives, and whether we deem it to be good or bad, we always know it's exactly where we are meant to be. Instead of flailing about on the winds of change, we find a sense of groundedness capable of carrying us through any storm. We can weather whatever is thrown at us when we know it is exactly what we are meant to be experiencing.

Because even those experiences we deem as bad help our soul to grow. When we know that we're aligned with our path, we don't have to resist what is happening and we don't get stuck in a chapter – instead, we allow the experience to transform us and carry us forth into the next unfolding chapter. When we align with our soul, we essentially put our soul in the body – we *embody* the soul – instead of forever chasing after it's desires. And we can live our lessons right now in this moment.

What if That, Too, Was Perfect?

Doing life right won't always look like flawless success and being completely unscathed. When we think that's what it's supposed to look like, we trap ourselves in a prison of our own making forever at odds with what is really happening in our own lives. But what if that, too, was perfect? The storm, the hardship, the pain?

Life is meant to have difficulties and pain that grow us, expand us, crack open our hearts – but we do not have to suffer. Feel? Yes. Suffer? No. We *are* meant to feel everything, painful and challenging as that may be. But feeling is what reminds us that we're alive.

However, we don't suffer when we know we're exactly where we're meant to be – when we're listening to the voice of our soul. And though our minds may feel confused at times, this wise voice within will never lead us astray.

Slowing Down

The first step in learning how to begin listening to your intuition is, you guessed it, slowing down. It's imperative to move from the fight-or-flight stress state to the parasympathetic "rest-and-digest" mode where we can actually hear our intuition.

It's quite challenging to access our intuition when we're stressed, and many of us live our lives in a chronic, low-grade fight-or-flight state. Luckily, we can move ourselves from fight-or-flight into the parasympathetic mode simply by changing our breathing.

Try it right now. Inhale slowly through your nose, feel like you're drawing that breath all the way down into your belly, and let your belly expand like a balloon. Then slowly exhale out through the nose, as you deflate your belly gently drawing your belly button inwards.

Now, do it again, but this time count to four as you inhale; then count to four, six, or eight as you exhale – whatever feels best to you. Then do that a total of ten times, inhaling and exhaling, in and out through the nose.

That's it. Do that same thing – breathing deeply in and out ten times – anytime you need to shift yourself back into the parasympathetic mode where you can access your intuition and make your wisest decisions.

Learn How Your Style of Intuition Shows Up

We don't all experience our intuition in the same way. So, it's important to become familiar with your particular brand and the unique way that your soul is sending you messages. Start to tune into the ways that your intuition sounds or feels, and where and how it shows up.

You might hear it, know it, feel it, or see it. Or you might experience a combination of these.

Hear it:

Do you ever hear a voice (no, you're not crazy) that almost sounds like your own? Maybe you've heard a warning voice keeping you from impending danger? Or you swear you've heard someone call your name even though no one else was around? Or you've heard a clear word or phrase drop into your awareness while meditating?

If so, lean into these experiences and become curious about them! There's a good chance this is your intuition trying to communicate with you, and all you need to do is listen.

Know it:

Do you tend to "just know" something but you're not sure how? Maybe you experience flashes of insight or those sudden *a-ha* moments, or experience downloads of complete chunks of information?

If that's the case, start to trust that sense of knowing! As we'll explore shortly, trusting that what we're receiving is valid and real can be the hardest part, but I'll give you some fun ways to start practicing.

Feel it:

Maybe you're someone who receives physical cues in the body. When you're weighing if a decision or an idea is right for you, do you tune into clues like whether it feels heavy or light, or experience shivers or chills, or have a strong gut feeling?

Those physical cues are more than mere sensations, they can be messages from your soul. This is where we get our saying "gut feeling" from, and it's more than just a saying, it's an actual experience of that!

See it:

Ever been told you have an "over-active" imagination? Maybe your dreams at night seem to be sending you messages about your life. Or do you easily daydream and see clear visions of your possible future?

These images that we often discount as mere figments of our imagination are ways that our intuition may be speaking to us. Start to play around with the idea that your imagination might actually be a powerful tool in your toolbox!

Building Trust

So, this is the hard part, right? Because there are so many conditioned barriers to trusting that inner soulful knowing. Most of us haven't received messaging that our intuition is a valid source of knowing. This is another symptom of our overly yang/masculine-energy culture where we are taught to exclusively listen to only half of our brain – the logical left-brain. And the messages we receive from our intuition aren't always going to be logical, rational and practical.

But the more you start to tune in and trust your intuition – in small ways at first – the easier it will become to hear, see, know, or feel it, and the harder it will become to disregard it. Use the practice that follows to begin building this trust!

-MAY PRACTICE-

SOULFUL INTUITIVE DECISIONS

During this month of springtime abundance, have fun experimenting with low-stakes intuitive decisions that connect you to your deep inner wisdom. Learn to make better, faster decisions infused with a sparkle of magic.

Step 1: Start Small

Start small and build up your ability to trust your intuition. Make low-stakes decisions first, where it doesn't matter if you're "wrong" – like which coffee mug to use in the morning, which tea to drink, what outfit to wear for the day, what color shoes to wear, which show or movie to watch, what to make for dinner, etc. It sounds silly, but it's the best way to start. And, it's fun.

Choose one of those categories above to practice with, or pick something else in your life that feels small and playful and that you have to make a daily decision about. Then for a whole week, practice by going with your *first flash of insight*.

Remember, that flash of insight might feel like an ah-ha moment that pops up into your mind, or it might be an image you clearly see in your mind's eye, or a word that you hear, or a feeling that pulls you towards something.

Your intuition might speak differently to you for different decisions, too. When I pick out a mug for my tea every morning, I usually get a feeling. When I choose what to wear each day, I see an image in my mind's eye. One mug will just feel *meh* and boring, while another one feels light and fun. I do the same with choosing which kind of tea to drink each morning. It sounds so funny and pointless because it's just a mug, right? It's just tea, who cares? But that's what makes it so fun to play around with. It brings a tiny sparkle of magic into my morning.

Maybe your mugs all look exactly the same and you drink the exact same tea or coffee every morning, so this wouldn't be a great practice for you! So, choose something that you do have to make a daily decision about, and see it as a way to bring a tiny sparkle of magic into your own day.

Choosing Books the Intuitive Way

A friend and I were recently comparing notes on how we choose our next books to read and discovered we both have a similar intuitive process that has really been improving things! I've personally always got a stack of books waiting to be read, as I buy them faster than I can read them. In the past, I would choose the next one based on something practical, like which book had been sitting there gathering dust the longest. But I would often find the book just wasn't grabbing me right then, and it was more of a struggle to want to read it. It had task energy written all over it.

So, one day I decided to choose a book from my big stack based on whatever I felt the most drawn to. When I opened it up, I was so surprised to see on the very first page something related to what I had just been thinking about in my own life. It was exactly what I needed to read at just the right time. And this happens time and time again now.

My friend Amanda reported that the same thing happens for her. She's often reading multiple books at one time – sometimes up to eight books – and says that she used to think she was just terrible at finishing books, with all these half-finished books lying around. But she started to trust her intuition to know which book to pick up when, and discovered the same experience – reading just the right words at exactly the right time.

Choosing a book isn't necessarily something that you need to make a daily decision about, but it's another fun and practical place to start honing your intuitive skills. And it's especially useful if you struggle to finish books and tend to feel bad about that – put it down until it intuitively calls to you again later, it's probably the perfect thing for your future self to read – or you tend to buy them faster than you can read them and need a foolproof method for choosing what's next.

Better and...Faster!

With time, you'll start to notice that making decisions this way – using your intuition – helps to not only facilitate better decisions...it also makes things a lot faster.

If you're someone who can overanalyze anything, this will speed up your decision-making process a lot. I could endlessly analyze all the pros and cons of each mug or tea in my cabinet based on a million factors each morning. And what to wear? Don't get me started.

When I started choosing my mug, my tea, and what to wear based on that first flash of insight, that feeling that pulls me towards one thing over another, those decisions now happen almost instantaneously, and always feel right. Better decisions. Faster decisions. Who doesn't want this?!

You can eventually practice making bigger and bigger decisions from this intuitive place, but start small to build up your confidence and skill.

I'm going to say it again – start small. Think of it like strengthening a muscle. I know you might be excited to jump in and go big right away, going for the most monstrous weight on the rack before you've worked your way up with all those dainty little weights first, but you're going to be able to build this as a sustainable and reliable skill when you start small and work your way up.

Have fun with the small decisions in the meantime! And be assured that they are laying down an important foundation for the long-term.

Step 2: Recognize the Barriers

When you start trying to listen to your intuition, you will likely notice the following barriers popping up and trying to override your intuitive knowing.

See if you recognize any of the following statements of limiting beliefs. If you're already familiar with your *cognitive functions*, which are the building blocks of the Myers Briggs system of personality, you can use those markers listed below (in the parentheses) as a guide, as our blocks and limiting beliefs are often closely tied to the particular way our brain is wired. If you're not familiar with the oft-forgotten cognitive functions, don't worry, you'll be getting a crash course in Chapter 5 during the month of July! For now, just read the following statements and see which ones you resonate with the most.

1. *It doesn't make logical sense.* (Often comes from Introverted Thinking).

2. *It doesn't seem like the effective path or it won't make any money – so we fear.* (Often comes from Extraverted Thinking).

3. *I can't even hear my intuition under a full bucket of emotional murkiness, or it's hard to decipher it from other strong feelings like fear.* (Often comes from Introverted Feeling).

4. *I think people will judge me for making that choice; I'm afraid what others will think, and afraid to disappoint others.* (Often comes from Extraverted Feeling).

5. *It doesn't lay out the whole path (because sometimes we receive insights as needed step by step).* (Often comes from Introverted Intuition).

6. *I don't believe the answer could be that simple or quick; I think it must be endlessly-analyzed to be right or true.* (Often comes from Extraverted Intuition).

7. *It's unconventional; it isn't the safe or known path.* (Often comes from Introverted Sensing).

8. *Listening to my intuition might mean that I can't have what I think I want right now.* (Often comes from Extraverted Sensing).

Have you heard some of these voices coming from your own mind before? Or from well-meaning family, friends, teachers, or society in general?

Many of them do seem like valid concerns. But that's why it's so important to start small when beginning to listen to your intuition. When you've been wearing blue all your life and you suddenly decide, *today I'm going to wear bold red!* and then your brain pops in and says, *how illogical! What will people think?!* It's a bit easier to say, *ah who cares about that, I'm going to do it anyway because it makes me feel good!*

If your first foray into trusting your intuition is something much bigger like deciding if you should quit your job or move across the country, you'll find it much harder to stand strong in the face of all those barriers that try to pop in and squash your great idea.

When you hear those other voices popping in – coming from your own mind or those around you – just notice them, say *thank you for your concerns*, and then gently, but firmly, let those voices know that you're going to try listening to your intuition this time instead.

Build up the muscle by keeping at it: you'll find that the more you listen to your intuition, the stronger and louder it gets.

Step 3: Accountability & Support

Reach out for accountability and support when you need it – a trusted friend, coach, mentor, or counselor who can help your mind release the fear it has in listening to a new source of wisdom. Tell them what you're doing and ask them to help keep you accountable when you're having a hard time quieting those voices above, or when you need a listening ear to talk it out.

Going Forward

Use these remaining few weeks of spring to start building up that muscle of intuition, by making those low-stakes intuitive decisions, and connecting to your soulful inner wisdom.

Remember: the mind is intelligent, but the soul is wise.

Recap: choose one of the low-stakes categories from Step 1 to practice with, or pick something else in your life that feels small and playful and that you have to make a daily decision about. Then for a whole week, practice by going with your *first flash of insight*. If you like how that feels, keep it going for another week, or maybe the whole month or beyond. Return to Steps 2 and 3 for troubleshooting and support when you need it.

And remember to have fun! Enjoy bringing a sparkle of magic into your mundane daily decisions. May you feel more and more aligned with the abundance and beauty of springtime as you watch your own life blossom!

PART II

SUMMER

Summer Intro:
The Good Life

AHH, SUMMER. WHERE I LIVE IN THE Midwest, summer isn't to be taken lightly. Many Minnesotans live their whole lives in eternal anticipation of our guaranteed three months of sunshine, lake time, and cabin adventures. It's a funny place to live if your favorite season is summer because we don't get that much of it; and yet its scarcity is exactly what seems to make it so sacred and sweet.

Summer is the season of *"full yang"* energy, a time of bright light, fiery heat, and heart-expanding joy. Our attention is fully outward, our adventures are in full swing, our hearts are in full-on connection mode. I think so many of us love the summer season because it naturally aligns with the energy we spend most of our time in. We are an overly "yang" culture in America – always *going, doing, achieving, pushing, striving.* And whether or not we believe this is actually good for us – it's familiar, it's comfortable.

But have you ever reached the end of the summer season, after a full-on sprint of *going and doing and socializing, and fiery heat and bright light and late nights* and felt – just a little bit...burned out? I know I have. As I started to tune more into the inner desires of my soul, rather than the external demands of society, I found just how much I needed slowness, quiet, and stillness. And I found I welcomed the arrival of fall with its promise of less doing and more – *being.*

Since we're committed to doing things differently this year, I challenge you to work on finding a bit of balance now, during the summer! By bringing just a bit of "yin" energy into this fully "yang" time of year – to truly feel the sacredness and sweetness of this bountiful season. And to redefine seeing "balance" as just a repeating series of sprints, burnouts and recoveries into something that's woven more deeply into the very fabric of our lives.

In June, as we officially transition from spring into summer, we'll work on staying grounded in the beauty and abundance of this time of year by tuning into the sweetness present in our own lives – even the drops of sweet nectar that can be found in the challenges.

Then in July, as we settle into this season of brightness and light, we'll celebrate and tune into our own personal brightness. And you'll be encouraged to shine your light even brighter in your own special way, as we explore the unique inner wiring and personality we each possess. As you discover a deeper level of understanding who and how you are, you'll find the joy and peace that accompany allowing yourself to finally live in alignment with your true soul nature.

And in August, as we start to feel that impending doom and dread of the coming fall and winter, and curse how quickly time flies, we'll examine our very relationship with time itself – this strict master that keeps us marching ever-forward at such a quick clip – and find ways to experience a slowness that expands and deepens each moment of our time.

May you enjoy a new experience of the summer season this year! One that doesn't simply fly by at a lightening pace, but instead grounds you into the slowness and abundance of every sweet moment.

CHAPTER 4

June:
Finding the
Sweetness

EVERY JUNE IN THE NORTHERN hemisphere we celebrate the Summer Solstice, the longest day of the year light-wise and the official first day of summer. The Summer Solstice is energetically a lot like a full moon – a time of culmination, celebration, reaching the peak, expansive growth, and big energy. We've done it! Climbed the mountain of light, reached the summit of brightness! Allow yourself to hang out here on top of the peak for a while – to celebrate, bask in the glow, and feel some gratitude for what has come to fruition.

But also know that eventually, we start the second half of the cycle, the descent. In moon terms, we would call that the waning cycle, from brightness to darkness. Just like a full moon, which symbolizes both celebration *and* release, the

Summer Solstice is the celebration of the light, as well as the release of it. One ending is always another beginning.

Darkness in the Summer?

We don't often think about the Summer Solstice symbolizing anything to do with darkness, because it's smack dab in the middle of the bright summer; but starting that day, we will make a slow return to darkness all the way until the Winter Solstice in late December. On the Winter Solstice, we then honor the darkness, as well as celebrate the return of the light.

It would be easy to think poorly of this half of the cycle. Nobody likes to think about the loss of light and the return to darkness, and it is certainly a faux pas where I live to even mention winter in the middle of the beloved summer.

But life isn't just about thriving in the good times, basking in the light, feeling joy and gratitude when everything is going our way. It's also about knowing how to find the sweetness, the beauty, the gratitude even during the hard times, the dark times, the times when things aren't going the way we would like them to.

But it's up to us to know HOW to do that. How to find the sweetness and beauty no matter the situation. And it's much easier to begin to strengthen this sweet-seeking muscle while things are bright and vibrant than to wait for the dark times and *then* try to convince ourselves to look for the good.

So, I encourage you to start working your sweet-seeking muscle right now, during this time of brightness and celebration! Keep reading and we'll get you flexing that muscle in no time at all.

What About the Truly Bad Times?

Also, know that this isn't a practice that is meant to keep you stuck in a situation that truly isn't serving your highest self by forcing you to find the good in it. We don't have to *stay* in every situation in order to find the good, or the growth, in it.

If we're in a situation that we know we must leave, like a job or a relationship that is no longer in our best interest, we have two choices. Option one – find the lesson, the growth, and then exit stage right. Take that kernel of good with you and leave the rest. Or option two – leave first, and then wait for a time in the future when you feel ready to retroactively look back at the situation and reflect on it in order to make peace with it and experience the growth from it.

Other times, we can't exit the situation – like an illness, or a rainy day, or a world pandemic. And sometimes exiting isn't even the point, or the goal. Like we've said before: *sometimes it's not about changing your life, sometimes it's about changing the way you experience your life.* There are so many soul lessons and so much heart-expanding growth to be had in the challenging times. But, oftentimes in this crazy world, even when we're trying our best to whether the storms, life can start to feel a little heavy, dark, overwhelming, or stale. But life is meant to be full of beauty and sweetness. We just have to learn to see it.

The Hummingbird: Master Sweet Seeker

The hummingbird is a fascinating creature. Though it is the smallest migrating bird, it doesn't let its size stop it as some will travel immense distances up to 4000 miles twice a year. And just to be uber tough-as-nails, it will complete this migration alone.

They are speedy – among the fastest fliers for their size, reaching speeds of 30-60mph.The only bird that can fly backwards, they are also extremely agile, able to make sudden movements up, down, and side to side effortlessly. They know nothing of slowness, as their name comes from the humming noise their wings make as they beat so fast – more than 50 times per *second*.

They stay extremely busy, visiting 1000-2000 flowers per day. Breathing 150 breaths per minute, they rarely stop to rest as they continue to hover in midair even while eating.

They are aggressive as they defend their food, and have big appetites. Eating 10-15 times per day, they feast almost exclusively on sugar in amounts that would be dangerous to other animals: flower nectar, tree sap, sugar water from feeders – and then just to avoid complete diabetes they balance this with additionally eating insects for protein.

So used to seeing hummingbirds in constant movement, we've even created a myth that hummingbirds will die if they stop moving. As humans we marvel at these tiny industrious creatures and think, WOW how can they even manage to stay alive?!

Now...let's be honest. Are you living the life of a hummingbird?

A tough-as-nails, I-can-do-it-all-myself-without-help approach to life?

Moving so fast through life you generate your own humming sound in your wake?

Never stopping to rest during the day – *not even while eating?*

Completing your own 1000-2000 tasks per day?

A nagging feeling that you, too, might die if you actually stop moving and doing?

Breathing so fast and shallow you're racking up anxiety and high blood pressure?

Just a little bit addicted to sugar?

I'm being silly, but I'm also...dead serious. Perhaps it's not in our best interest to model our lifestyle after such an inexplicable little creature! Or, perhaps we've just honed in on the wrong qualities *to* model ourselves after. Because there is one thing that Hummingbird does better than any other creature, and it's something we certainly could use more of in our own lives: finding the sweetness in life.

When We Stop Looking for the Sweetness

As part of its very survival strategy the hummingbird must look for the beauty and sweetness in life. It can starve to death in 3-5 hours. All of the other hardships and extreme qualities present in its existence aren't what's going to kill it. But if it stops looking for beauty and sweetness, it will die. Interesting lesson to ponder, right? What happens in our own lives when we stop looking for the beauty and sweetness?

We've learned that we have the power to change our world by changing our perception. If you expect the world to be harsh and people to be bad, this is what you will see. But if you expect to see the beauty in the world and the sweetness in each other, you will find *that* to be true, as well.

We are co-creators of our reality – we always get to choose our perception. What do you choose to perceive? There is no shortage of bad news to perceive, we don't need any help there. But what about the good? What if you just have to look a little closer? Listen a little harder? Perceive just a little deeper underneath the surface of what we're told to believe?

> *"Be soft.*
> *Do not let the world make you hard.*
> *Do not let pain make you hate.*
> *Do not let the bitterness steal your sweetness.*
> *Take pride that even though the rest of the world may*
> *disagree,*
> *you still believe it to be*
> *a beautiful place."*

> -Iain S. Thomas[15]

The Secret to Finding the Sweetness

My uncle Ray passed away a few years ago unexpectedly. If there's one thing I learned from him over the years, it was the power of living with joy. There's a reason so many of us referred to him as Ray of Sunshine. When down in Florida going through some of my uncle's belongings with my dad, amongst all of his famous brightly patterned colorful shirts, I found this beautiful hanging glass with a phrase engraved upon it:

The earth has music for those who listen.[16]

Perhaps there was a reason he was always so joyful. It seems he knew the secret. The secret to finding the sweetness: that life is good for those who know how to live. There's a story I've always loved shared by philosophy writer Laurence G. Boldt about a peasant who leaves his small hometown and goes out to explore the world. Upon returning, his fellow villagers are curious to know what life is like in the rest of the world. To which the traveler replies, *"same as here. It is good for those who know how to live."*[17]

What is this "knowing how to live?" I think a big part of it is knowing that sweetness doesn't always just appear; sometimes you have to look deeper. Sometimes you have to listen harder. If we take a what-you-see-is-what-you-get approach to life, we are destined to miss it. But if we look just below the surface, it is there. The sweet nectar of life. The beauty, the goodness, the music.

Sweetness and Gratitude Work Together

There is a similar quality to gratitude. We tend to think it is something that just happens to us, that we must wait around for that blessed moment when we truly feel grateful. That we must wait for the winds of life to shift in order to experience the beauty and sweetness of life. My friend, if you wait – you will be waiting for a very long time.

Instead, what if you try out one of the secrets of those who "know how to live" and work on generating a little sweetness and gratitude right now? Sweetness and gratitude work together. Just for a moment, imagine that you are the hummingbird. Imagine that finding beauty and sweetness is essential to your wellbeing, to your very survival and existence, and that you need a new hit of sweetness every 10-15 minutes.

Ok, so you're soaring through the air close to the surface so you can keep an eye on your sources of beauty and sweetness. You spot the most beautiful flower, you lock your perception on it, and boom – you zip down and lap up the sweetness. What now? What else but gratitude? Gratitude, relief, peace, contentment, joy.

You have ten minutes. Begin seeking your next hit of beauty.

Did you get the metaphor? We don't need to just *imagine* that beauty and sweetness are essential to our wellbeing and existence, they are! Just in the less literal sense. But if you find the metaphorical sweetness severely lacking in your own life, yet you're constantly reaching for literal sweetness in the form of a sugar addiction – you might want to ponder the correlation! We will seek sweetness in our lives one way or another.

It's Not a Talent or a Trait, It's a Practice

Begin to hone your own radar for beauty and sweetness. Imagine if you, too, could move through the world with a fine-tuned sweet-seeking radar. Imagine how difficult it would be to miss all the good that is truly happening. A single flower is easy to miss in a whole world. But somehow the hummingbird finds it. You can too.

One of the best ways to start shifting your powers of perception is through a practice of gratitude. Just like in the practice of mindfulness, there is a formal and an informal practice. When learning mindfulness meditation, you must commit to the formal practice – the sitting your butt down and doing nothing but meditating part – in order for that to then influence the informal practice, the part where you start to move through the world more mindfully, less reactively, more attuned to each moment no matter the task at hand.

But without that formal practice, the informal is hard to attain. This is the same with gratitude. We often try to embody the informal practice before we've ever attempted the formal practice. And then we wonder why we're not that good at it, or why it's so unattainable, or why those moments of sweetness are so far and few in between.

It's simple. Can you be a master mathematician if you never practice math? Can you be a grateful sweet-seeking human being if you never practice gratitude? Because I know how easy it is to put off starting a practice of gratitude, and I know how quickly the logical brain will barge in and declare it silly or inauthentic or pointless, let's not even wait – let's begin right now.

-JUNE PRACTICE-

BECOMING A SWEET-SEEKING BEING

As we officially transition from spring into summer, keep yourself grounded in the beauty and abundance of this time of year by tuning into the sweetness present in your own life – even the drops of sweet nectar that can be found in the challenges.

As you move through each of the following exercises, it's helpful to notice where in your body you feel the feeling of gratitude. Is it just a thought in your head? Is it an emotion you feel in your heart? Is it a bodily sensation like warmth or tingling? Notice what gratitude feels like to you.

We'll start off easy.

1.   THINK OF SOMETHING GOOD IN YOUR LIFE...

Don't make it too complicated. There is always something good whether it's the delicious breakfast you ate, or having enough money to have food on your table, or it's a job that you love or a squooshy faced pet to snuggle with, etc – whatever is true in your life. And then say out loud, feel internally, or write down: **I am so grateful for (fill in the blank).**

Let's pause a moment while you actually do this. Don't say, I'll come back to this later when I can really focus on it! Don't wait for the "perfect" moment. Do it now. This one will only take you 10 seconds. We will wait for you.

2.   NOW THINK OF SOMEONE YOU LOVE IN YOUR LIFE...

All kinds of love apply here: partners, family members, friends, mentors, pets if you didn't already cover them in the above! And then say out loud, feel internally, or write down: **I am so grateful for (fill in the blank).**
Pause and do this.

3.   NEXT THINK OF YOUR FAVORITE ASPECT OF NATURE...

Maybe it's the warm sun, the beautiful flowers, the ancient trees, the soft grass, the stunning moon, staring up at the clouds, etc. And then say out loud, feel internally, or write down: **I am so grateful for (fill in the blank).**

Got it? Ok that wasn't too hard, right?! It's helpful to remind ourselves that there is always some sweetness present if we stop and notice.

So, let's make it more challenging. This is where we really work that sweet-seeking muscle.

4.   THINK OF A CHALLENGE IN YOUR LIFE...

This could be past or present – maybe it's the loss of a job, the loss of a loved one, a health issue or crisis, something that feels like a lack or a challenge. And now think of what you're grateful for within that situation.

It's harder, right? I'll give you some examples to get your sweet-seeking muscle warmed up, plus some tips below that for how to make it feel genuine:

EXAMPLE #1 – Abundance doesn't always mean money. If you've lost your job, what do you currently have an abundance of? *Time?* Time to sit outside with a good cup of tea, breathe deeply, and enjoy nature while you look for new jobs online? *Space?* Space to finally do what you really want to do with your life?

EXAMPLE #2 – If you've lost someone from your life, whether through death or separation, what has the experience given you? A deeper appreciation for the time you still have left here? The laughter and love you shared with this person that deeply enriched your life?

EXAMPLE #3 – I once found myself in the hospital facing near-emergency surgery on my intestines. Three surgeries, actually. On the surface, this seemed very bad and very challenging. But I also felt a great sense of relief. Relief and gratitude that I no longer had to follow the incredibly strict "healing protocol" that wasn't working for me anyway. It was so constricting and all-consuming, but my perfectionist attitude wouldn't let me give it up. Thrown in the hospital by means outside of my control, I finally felt like I could breathe again. I always remember that exact moment. I remember the relief and the gratitude and then thinking, *is it weird that I feel relief and gratitude that I'm in the hospital?* Maybe. But it was those little bits of gratitude that got me through the whole ten-month experience.

Now it's your turn – think of that past or present challenging time in your life and the piece of it that you are grateful for and say out loud, feel internally, or write down: **I am so grateful for (fill in the blank).**

Tips to Make it Feel Genuine:

If it feels contrived or inauthentic or pointless, the trick is to make it *genuine*. Don't try to convince yourself that you're grateful for something that you're not. Dive a little deeper and find the nectar, the little bit of sweetness that you ARE grateful for, whatever that may be.

Yes, you can still feel that the whole entire challenging situation absolutely sucked! You're not trying to delude yourself; you're just identifying the drop of sweetness, naming it, and using it to thrive. There were some days in the hospital that all I could muster to write down in my gratitude journal was, *I am so grateful for my life-sustaining breath.* And that was true and genuine.

Take a pause here for a moment so you can complete this.

5. **LET'S KEEP IT GOING. NOW THINK OF SOMEONE IN YOUR LIFE WHO FRUSTRATES OR CHALLENGES YOU...**

We all have that person, or many people! And then think of one thing you DO appreciate about them as a person, OR the lesson the relationship has taught you.

For example, I have had some challenging times in relationships of all varieties that have shown me that I truly don't have to outsource my power or my sense of self to others, and that I can get that from within my own self. Can you imagine going through all of life never getting the chance to learn that? For this I am grateful. We need challenging people in our lives to push us to grow. It's what turns us from a stagnant piece of coal into a bright and shiny diamond.

So, think of this person that has played a role in your polishing, and think of what it is you're grateful for about them or what that relationship has taught you, and then say out loud, feel internally, or write down: **I am so grateful for (fill in the blank).**

We'll pause here while you do this.

6. **OK LAST ONE, YOU'RE DOING AWESOME. LET'S MAKE IT FUN. THINK OF A GLOOMY DAY (STAY WITH ME HERE ON THE FUN PART)...**

Then think of what you're truly grateful for when the weather is crummy and you have to stay inside. I know, it's hard. I'm a Minnesotan and we're hard-wired to be obsessed with "good weather." But is it the chance to cuddle up with a favorite book and a cup of tea? The rare opportunity to do nothing? The helpful reminder that darkness is just part of life's cycles, whether it's outside in nature or in your own life? The knowing that the rain makes everything vibrant again and brings the rainbow?

Think about how fun the next rainy day is going to feel with your newfound awareness, and then say out loud, feel internally, or write down: **I am so grateful for (fill in the blank)!**

Going Forward

There, you did it. You officially completed your first formal practice of gratitude and are well on your way to being a stellar sweet-seeking being. Keep up the formal practice by returning to this daily. It doesn't have to be ALL of these questions every day. Choose one or two each time. Make it short and...yes, sweet.

Any consistent gratitude practice is better than none at all, especially when you're first building up that muscle. Eventually it just becomes a natural way of perceiving the world. But at first, you've got to make yourself do it. I love this practice so much that I still keep up the formal version of writing in a gratitude journal daily, and have been doing so for nearly ten years.

I highly recommend making a consistent time of day when you can do this, like first thing in the morning, or last thing before going to bed at night. Make it a part of your morning or evening routine, just like brushing your teeth or washing your face. This is spiritual hygiene at its finest.

Or create a new routine, like during your afternoon break at work. What a great way to infuse a little sweetness into your work day, especially in the afternoon when we start to hit that slump. Grab a cup of tea and your gratitude journal and set a timer for 5-10 minutes.

Short and Sweet

A note on size: when it comes to the size of your gratitude journal, I can't stress enough the importance of using a very small journal. Or breaking up a larger page into short sections of just a few lines for each day. We want this to be something you actually do – every day or close to every day – and not something that feels like a big task you have to schedule into your busy week. Because then, you won't do it. And we want to do this!

Instead of a journal, you can also do this with a jar. Get a big jar and a bunch of colorful post-it notes, and every day write your gratitude on a little note and toss it into the jar. You can get creative decorating the jar if that's your jam, and it's a cool visual to see your jar getting filled up with all that goodness and sweetness in your life. Don't get too hung up on making this project perfect and never getting started though; the important part is that you start.

Remember, hummingbird *dies* without sweetness. What part of you dies without sweetness in your life? Your soul or spirit? Eek. This is essential to your wellbeing. Because life is meant to be full of beauty and sweetness. We just have to learn to see it.

Keep this short and sweet practice up for the month of June, and then assess and see how you feel. You just might decide that it's essential enough to keep it going beyond this month!

May you always know how to find the beauty in the darkness, the gratitude in the hard times, the sweetness in the challenges. Sending love and gratitude to my fellow hummingbirds; here's to becoming a master sweet-seeker in your own life!

CHAPTER 5

July: Shining Your Bright Light

ARRIVING ON THE HEELS OF THE Summer Solstice, July is a time for basking in summer's peak of brightness and light. In the astrological calendar, the sun will also cross over into Leo season this month. Leo is the lion, a sign of bold confidence. Supported by this energy, this is the time of year when we can feel most confident about stepping out into the light and sharing our true selves with the world, letting people see our true personality!

But sometimes...*just being ourselves* can have unexpected consequences when we don't fit the perfect social mold. Or maybe, even figuring out WHO we truly are doesn't seem so straightforward.

When the World Doesn't Like Your Personality

I love this scene from the movie *Ride the Eagle*; it's a phone conversation between characters Leif and Gorka, played by Jake Johnson and Luis Fernandez-Gil:

> *"The band wants you out, and I can't believe it."*
> *"What?!"*
> *"It's not personal. It's just...your style, your energy, your vibe – and your personality – doesn't fit in."*
> *"My personality, Gorka? How is that not personal? It's MY personality!"*[18]

Well...we've all been there before, right? That feeling that somehow, we just don't fit in. When I was little, I was super shy in school. I was great at making friends in a one-on-one situation, but I wanted to die every time the teacher threatened to spontaneously call on someone. Even though I was a straight-A student, I remember parent-teacher conferences always mentioning how I could "participate" more. In college, I got my first and only C in a class called *Changing the World* because the teacher graded heavily on "participation," which meant raising your hand and opening your mouth. It didn't matter if you could write well, or how deep or accurate the thoughts in your head were. It mattered if you could open your mouth and you know, say those thoughts, out loud.

There is some logic and usefulness there! But too often, racking up those participation points meant simply opening your mouth and saying literally anything. I spent a lot of my schooldays looking around and wondering why the world valued so heavily being able to open your mouth and say words, despite the accuracy, validity, or relevancy of those words to the conversation.

I also envied those kids who could raise their hands so confidently, say something – right or wrong – and rack up those participation points. It seemed to come so easily to them. The thought of being heard, or being wrong, god forbid, barely a concern at all. For me, the thought of raising my hand was terrifying, and my arm remained heavily glued to my side, my eyes averted from the teacher's radar, while envisioning my body melting into the chair.

I remember classroom presentations with my voice shaking and my cheeks blazing red. Being called on and my mind going completely blank with everyone staring at me – the kind kids urging me to *just say anything* so the painful awkwardness would stop. And then there were the voice tests in choir class where I was expected to sing alone and would panic to the point of producing sounds that I'm pretty sure couldn't be classified as actual musical notes based on the confused look on the teacher's face. Though I've become much more comfortable with many of these facets as I've gotten older and found my own ways of going about them, it's still a big part of who and how I am.

The Desperate Act of Fitting In

Susan Cain, author of the book that started a movement, *Quiet: The Power of Introverts in a World That Can't Stop Talking,* is a huge advocate for bringing the concept of introversion into our collective consciousness and giving it the recognition it deserves as a legitimate way of being – and not as something we must "overcome." She says,

> "Introversion – along with its cousins sensitivity, seriousness, and shyness – is now a second-class personality trait, somewhere between a disappointment and a pathology. Introverts living under the Extrovert Ideal are like women in a man's

world, discounted because of a trait that goes to the core of who they are. Extroversion is an enormously appealing personality style, but we've turned it into an oppressive standard to which most of us feel we must conform."[19]

It was a long time before I heard the term *"introvert,"* and even longer before I encountered the concept of *"sensitivity."* The trait of sensitivity was discovered by researcher Elaine Aron and discussed in depth in her book, *The Highly Sensitive Person: How to Thrive When the World Overwhelms You.* This largely genetic trait occurs naturally in approximately 20% of humans – and is found in over 100 other species, as well – and impacts the sensitivity of the nervous system in ways that produce both gifts and challenges. [20]

I guess I did *hear* the term "introvert" in college while majoring in psychology, but I didn't actually *resonate* with it at that time in my life because I was trying so hard to embody the Extrovert Ideal. But oh, what a farce that was. Sure, the introduction of alcohol, with its wondrous ability to numb some of those pesky introverted and sensitive parts, made me the perfect social butterfly at college parties. And a general discomfort of being alone with myself, as well as a bound determination to appear "normal," kept my social calendar busy from breakfast to sundown. I was pretty pleased with my efforts to fit in – but I couldn't keep it up forever.

Is This Who I Really Am?

When I was diagnosed with Crohn's disease at age 26, everything changed. I worked with a naturopathic doctor and followed a ton of dietary restrictions, including cutting out everything from gluten to dairy to sugar to alcohol. I still remember going to a Halloween party shortly after that, dressed as Catwoman. Sitting alone, as the only sober party-goer in the corner of a dance floor wearing cat ears and feeling more awkward than ever, I had plenty of time to contemplate, *is THIS who I really am?!* When you strip away everything else, am I just an awkward cat in the corner? Good god.

A few more years would have to pass before I finally got to the point where I would lovingly joke that one of my favorite hobbies was maintaining white space on my calendar. I was starting to love the space in between, the downtime, the quiet moments – and beginning to realize just how much I needed it to not be a crazy, angry, sick person. I was realizing that I had to let go of trying to fit in, and instead embrace being who I truly was.

Sure…it took moving to a new state where I knew no one; having Crohn's disease that sapped much of my energy; being stuck in a hospital and alone much of the time for nearly six weeks; having a spiritual and emotional epiphany; and finally meeting a new friend who opened my eyes to a deeper and more nuanced world of personality types where I could finally see my true self reflected back to me…but I finally found my way back to my true nature. And I learned to love my quiet, slow-moving, deep, sensitive self – despite the world telling us that we should be otherwise.

There's a lot of nuance that goes into the makeup of who and how we are, and these are just some of the individual facets of who and how I am. There are just as many unique facets that make up who and how you are. In the end, the most important part is that no matter who and how we are *at our core*, that we allow ourselves to live and act in alignment with that.

How to Save Your Life: Be Yourself

Recently I had the pleasure of listening to one of the most fascinating stories that reiterates just how essential it is to live in alignment with our true selves. Not only essential, but *life-saving.*

After battling cancer for four years, Anita Moorjani fell deep into a coma. Her organs shutting down, her body riddled with tumors, she wasn't expected to make it through the night. But in this state, she had an experience of going to the "other side" before choosing to return again to her body. To the amazement of the medical community, after returning from her near-death experience and regaining consciousness from the coma, her advanced stage cancer began to rapidly heal. Within weeks she was completely free of cancer.

What happened? Moorjani says that while on the other side, she had the realization that she hadn't been truly loving and caring for herself; she hadn't been allowing herself to live as her true authentic self. Prior to her cancer diagnosis, she spent a lot of time being a people-pleaser, seeking approval, and *"trying really hard to be a good spiritual person."* But the near-death experience taught her that, *"we don't have to work at being spiritual, we ARE spiritual"* – and she now realizes that it's not about figuring out how to be the best spiritual person, but instead asking the questions, *"Who am I? What is my authentic self?"*

She went on to say that we're so conditioned to believe we're not good enough, that we have to be someone else – but that, *"when you don't allow yourself to be who you are, you don't allow the Divine to express through you. You're blocking the channel."*[21] And when we block the channel, that source of love and light and healing, we get sick.

When I heard her story that day, I resonated with it so much. And felt validated that what I've come to believe about the connection between our authentic self-expression and the health of our body, is true. Because my experience with illness taught me the same lesson. I thought I had tried everything to cure myself of Crohn's disease – I would try just about *anything,* and spent five years desperately trying to avoid surgery and life-long infusion medications. I worked with naturopaths, acupuncturists, energy healers. I underwent food sensitivity testing, made huge dietary changes, and took copious amounts of supplements. I had my gut tested for all sorts of imbalances, consulted with western doctors, and took short-term courses of conventional medications.

But in the final twist of fate, when I had been precisely following an extremely strict autoimmune dietary plan that I hoped would cure me as it seemingly had for others, the disease instead flared with a vengeance and I ended up in the hospital with a perforated intestine, an abscess so large it had its own medical name, moving quickly to avoid sepsis and bone infection, and facing yes, surgery and long-term medications.

As I recovered from each of the three intestinal surgeries over the course of nine months, I continued to complete the 700-hours of holistic nutrition studies I had previously begun. During an earlier peak of success when nutritional changes had temporarily put the disease into remission, I had felt inspired to work with others in the same way. But I became discouraged in my heart that the path of nutrition had seemingly failed me in the end. I still graduated with honors from the program, yet instead of forging ahead as I originally intended, I paused, I waited, and I listened.

I started to feel a clear message deep down that nutrition – while fascinating, life-changing, and still able to help so many – wasn't the end of my personal healing path, and it wasn't the end of what I could teach to others. I realized that I was still passionate about what we feed ourselves, but that the definition of "feeding ourselves" had changed for me. I became passionate about all the ways that we truly feed ourselves – not just the quality of the food we put in our bodies, but the way we feel about that food; our stress levels and the ways that we help nourish and balance ourselves; our ability to connect to our heart and our sense of joy; and our deeper understanding and appreciation of our unique selves. I began to understand that I, too, still had much deeper work to be done.

Doing the Deeper Work

Each one of us is a culmination of our physical body, our mind, our heart and emotions, as well as our energetic makeup including our soul and our spirit. By starting with the most subtle, inner aspects of understanding myself and working outward from there, I began to:

- Understand my unique needs and innermost desires on a soul level.
- Explore my connection to my heart, and my ability to feel and express my emotions.
- Develop an awareness of my mind and my pattern of thoughts.
- Discover new routines, habits and solutions that supported my body and my whole self in my day-to-day happiness and health.

A lot of these answers came from examining myself for the first time through the lens of personality, or more accurately, Psychological Type (which we'll explore together in this month's practice) to discover how my brain was wired, and to understand who and how I really was behind all the layers of expectations about how we are "supposed" to be. This time, the solutions I employed were simpler, more joy-focused, and more aligned with who I really am.

I had tried too hard for too long to put together my puzzle using only some of the pieces, but all of that began to change. We can't put a puzzle back together using only some of the pieces – much as we can't expect to find true healing by examining only some of our many parts.

Your Personality is a Tool

I believe that your soul chose your personality to help you carry out your life mission here. It's an important tool at your disposal – but you have to know how to use the tool. And this is definitely not about putting ourselves or others into a box – we are not meant to be slaves to our personality. The personality serves *us*.

But we have to be very clear about what we are even talking about here. There is a big difference between what we often think of as our personality, or our conditioned behaviors, versus our true nature, or true *Self*. Our conditioned behaviors make up the roles we play and the masks we wear to better fit in with our society and the many expectations that are placed upon us about who we are supposed to be. These behaviors are the culmination of everything that has happened to us in our lives, and the adaptations we've created to best deal with that.

Whereas our true nature, or capital-S *Self*, is the personality underneath all of the adaptations and the expectations, the original wholeness we were born with. You might say it's the personality of your soul. But to get to that core part of who we are, we first have to learn to let go of everything that is *not* us. Everything that is keeping us small, stuck, sick, or less than. We have to learn to let go of the layers of expectations – the expectations placed upon us from the ideals of society and our family, the expectations from school and our jobs, the expectations inherent in our gender and the roles we play such as mother, father, husband, wife, as well as roles like good-citizen, perfectionist, or people-pleaser.

This is a process of growth, and shedding all the accumulated layers of "not-Self" doesn't happen overnight. But as we begin to see glimpses of and remember ourselves at the level of our true nature, we start to cultivate the energy of self-acceptance, self-love, and self-permission – vital energies needed to allow our soul to express itself freely. And as we let go of guilt, shame, self-hatred, and fear, we discover that underneath all of that – lives who we really are, minus the wounds and the defenses and the expectations and the adaptations.

It is the true you.

How to (Actually) Change the World

And yes, underneath all of those layers, at the deepest core of who we are, we are love and light. Just like this person, and that person, and every single person on this whole entire Earth. I think it's a beautiful thing to realize how truly similar we are. But I also think it's a beautiful thing to realize how we are *different*. Because those differences are how we change the world. Those differences hold the specific gifts of our soul given to us to equip each of us with the skills we need to accomplish our mission here on Earth. To hopefully make this Earth a more beautiful place to live.

While I may have gotten the worst grade of my academic career in a class called *Changing the World* because I didn't live up to the Extrovert Ideal, I can now confidently say I am eons closer to changing the world than I ever was in that class – by being *more* of my sensitive, introverted self. Not less! If we were all exactly the same, how could we solve all of the many varied and nuanced problems that plague us in our world? Thank goodness for our differences, for right now we need everyone's gifts at full strength on the table ready to go. We need loud powerful voices *and* quiet deep thoughts; we need fast action *and* slow living; we need out-of-the-box thinkers *and* feelers with big hearts; we need imagineers and dreamers, and builders and makers, we need the movers and the shakers. We truly need them all!

My friend Lauren likes to jokingly say that we're not all meant to become so similar that we're just a greige blob *(greige – an actual official color that blends the best of the dullest grey and beige)*. And I love that reminder, because while tearing down the walls that divide us and the distinctions that keep us separate *is* big work to be done in the world right now, and we *do* need to remember how similar we are – we also need to see, appreciate, and love how we are different. Not the differences at the level of our conditioning that take us further and further away from our true nature – but the differences at the level of our soul.

A rainbow isn't just one color, but a beautiful spectrum of many versions of the same light. We must learn to LOVE who we are and how we are wired. And also, to love how our fellow beings are wired. When we do this, we give others permission to be themselves – to be their own version of their wild and perfect wiring. We stop holding others hostage to some set of expectations that isn't right for them – and maybe isn't even right for us! In freeing ourselves, we also free those around us. In giving ourselves permission, we also give permission to others.

It's a soul-sucking energy trying to grow from a place of: *I'm not ok, not enough, there is something wrong with me and I must cram my star-shaped self into this bland square in order to be loved, liked, and accepted.* Versus growing and expanding ourselves from the place of: *I am perfect and enough, AND I can continue to learn, work on myself, and grow into an even grander expression of myself!* It still takes work to grow from this place, but it's drawing life-giving energy *to* us rather than draining our life force by trying to become something we are not.

There are treasures stored in our personality – our natural, and sometimes hidden, talents that we can nurture into powerhouse skillsets if we give ourselves permission to. And there are inherent weaknesses within our unique personality – that probably won't become our greatest skillsets no matter how hard we try. However, far from being something we should simply ignore, our weaknesses point to the areas we can cultivate just enough of to experience greater balance, playfulness, stability, and wholeness. On the journey to our center we can find, and work with, both our shadow and our light. If we dig deep enough, we can even discover what our soul yearns to bring into this world via examining our longings and aspirations, sometimes sneakily veiled under what we both envy or loathe in others. Sometimes it takes a bit of creativity to figure out just how to accomplish these aspirations, but I assure you that you're equipped with just the right set of gifts and tools to get the job done.

And how does this change the world? We can see our answer in what theologian and social activist Howard Thurman has famously said: *"Don't ask what the world needs. Ask what makes you come alive and go do it. Because what the world needs is people who have come alive."*[22]

The Missing Piece of Healing

For me, discovering a deeper nuanced world of personality types wasn't a way to put myself into a comfortable box – it was a way to smash the box that was full of the expectations of how we are "supposed" to show up in the world. It was a way to shed the skins I'd been wearing that were two sizes too tight, a way to release the heavy weight of trying to be something and someone I am not.

For me, this world of personality types was the missing piece in my own healing journey where nothing else had been working. It was a tool to show me, me. A mirror to reflect back who, on some level, I already knew I was meant to be. Because when we say things like, *hey you just gotta be your true authentic self!* – do we even know what that means? Sometimes we're so far from who we are at our core that we need a little help to remember, we need a map to guide us back to center.

I also knew that this nuanced version of personality types was the missing piece in how I wanted to work with clients throughout their own healing journeys. Throughout my experience of trying to cure myself of Crohn's disease, I found that even in the world of holistic healthcare there can sometimes be a similarity to the western medical model. It can be the same old approach, just different tools: *here's the disease, here's the protocol.* Instead of medications, here's a bunch of supplements. Instead of, *who are you and what's really going on in your world*, it's how can you fit yourself into this specific protocol? Oftentimes, we're still just treating the symptoms. And neglecting to examine the role of the heart, mind and soul. But no more to the one-size-fits-all approach, to the protocols that treat a disease instead of a person, and to the brown bags full of so many medications and supplements that we can't even keep track anymore. No more to external-only approaches that completely forget about a pretty key piece of healing: YOU. While every tool has its time and place on a healing journey, medications and supplements included, what I discovered I especially wanted to know about myself and my clients is: **who are you?**

> *What is your personality type? How is your brain wired?*
>
> *How is your heart? Do you process your emotions? Where are you storing unprocessed emotions? What are you carrying around in your energy body?*
>
> *How is your soul? What are the lessons you are here to learn?*
>
> *Is who and how you are in alignment with society's expectations of how we are "supposed" to be? If not, what does that mean for you – how does that make you feel, and how do you find where you fit?*
>
> *Are you living in or out of alignment with who and how you are?*

Because all of these pieces are so key in whether the body manifests in disease or health.

Living Your Purpose

When we start asking these questions about who we are, we also find that we tend to stumble upon our purpose. What follows *who are you?* is often the second question, *why are you here?* What is your soul's purpose? Why did you come here? What are you meant to accomplish? And if your soul chose your personality as a tool to best accomplish your goals here, it's a great place to begin searching for clues to that illusive question about our true mission or purpose.

But if we build our lives from the outside in, layered upon our *conditioned personality* and the role we are trying to play or the societal ideal we are trying to live up to – we will always feel like something is missing. There will always be a sense that something is keeping us stuck, sick, or small. The trick is to instead build your life from the inside out – layered upon the personality of your *true nature* – in order to become who you really are: bright, whole, and deeply fulfilled.

Heal the Soul and the Body Will Follow

According to the standard medical model, Anita Moorjani's body should have died – from cancer, numerous tumors, and her organs shutting down. But her soul had an otherworldly experience, returned, and her body inexplicably healed. A medical marvel. She doesn't believe that it was the cancer that nearly killed her. She says that *"the cancer saved her life;"* that it was SHE who was killing herself.

I resonate with this in my own journey, too. It wasn't Crohn's disease trying to wreak havoc on my body. It was ME wreaking havoc on my body – and on my mind and my heart and my soul. It was perfectionism that was killing me; it was disconnection from my true self that was killing me; it was people-pleasing and fear; it was resentment and frustration; it was being a doormat, and saying yes when I meant no; it was not trusting myself, not understanding my needs, not listening to my intuition – and not giving myself permission to be 100% who and how I am at the level of my soul.

I believe that the health of our body is intimately tied to this idea of expressing our true authentic self. The motto for my healing and coaching business reflects this concept – *heal the soul and the body will follow; support the body so the spirit has room to dance.*

I envision a world where each and every one of us is encouraged to live authentically from a place of true self. And in so doing radiates joy, truth and authenticity outward, allowing every cell of the body, mind, and emotions to align in health. May you use the practices this month to begin discovering these deeper layers of who you really are, and enjoy turning up the volume on your light, and your health!

-JULY PRACTICE-

THIS IS YOUR BRAIN ON YOU

As we settle into this season of brightness and light, enjoy celebrating and tuning into your own personal brightness! Explore the unique inner wiring and personality that you possess, and discover an even deeper level of self-love and understanding.

Fun Brain Facts: Did You Know?

For introverts living in a society that values the Extrovert Ideal, finally resting into your true introverted nature can be a huge a-ha and a big step in the right direction of living from your true soul self – as I discovered for myself and shared in this month's chapter.

But extroverts, here's something fun for you, too, that can be a big step in understanding who and how YOU truly are! Maybe you're an extrovert who's never really resonated with being an extrovert, because the definition of extroversion is often too narrowly defined. We tend to assume that all extroverts look the same, but did you know that there are actually four different kinds of extroversion? That means that some extroverts don't look like the stereotypical social butterfly that we've come to associate with the definition of extroversion. Likewise, there are four different kinds of introversion, as well.

Renowned Swiss psychiatrist Carl Jung first hypothesized this theory in 1921 in his book *Psychological Types*,[23] and now modern neuroscience, such as the fascinating EEG brain imaging work by Dr. Dario Nardi, backs this up by showing these different mental processes occurring in different brains.[24] We'll be exploring these eight mental processes – four kinds of extroversion and four kinds of introversion – as part of this month's practice.

Just to clarify, according to Jung it is technically spelled "extrAversion," but over time we started spelling it "extrOversion," possibly just to match the spelling of introversion. But "extra" means "outside" in Latin, meaning extraverts turn outward; similarly, "intro" means "inside" in Latin, referring to introverts turning inward. Either spelling is fine, but just a heads up that I'll now be using the technical spelling "extravert."

For the Ambiverts...Let's Clear This One Up

While we're on the subject of introversion and extraversion, I know some of you will be thinking, well that's all well and good, *but I'm an ambivert.*

So, what's an ambivert? It's a term that I both love and hate. "Ambi" in Latin means "both." So, it's a term meant to imply that there are some people who, unlike the introverts and extraverts, are in a third separate category because they possess traits of both of these types. But guess what? In all actuality, we are ALL ambiverts.

In an extravert's brain, the primary mental process that is favored will be an extraverted process – one that connects the person to the outer world. So, they get their energy from interaction with the outer world. But the secondary process favored by an extravert's brain will be an introverted process – that connects the person to their own inner world. An extravert having a connection to their inner world helps them to be a balanced human being.

And in an introvert's brain, it's just the opposite – they favor a primary mental process connecting them to their own inner world, which is where they will get their energy from. But they utilize a secondary mental process that connects them to the outer world, which helps them to be a balanced human being.

It's a good thing we have access to both sides of ourselves – our inner and outer worlds. Can you imagine an introvert that literally couldn't interact with another human being, or an extravert that literally couldn't access their own ideas, thoughts, feelings, or memories? Sure, we might struggle with some of these aspects more than others, but we all *can* do both. If you see yourself as an "ambivert," you are probably spending more equal time using both your primary and secondary mental processes.

So, the word "ambivert" is a great term that reminds us that no one is entirely all introvert or all extravert, but it gets used incorrectly by implying that there's an entirely separate group of people for which this is true.

No one is an ambivert, AND we're all ambiverts!

Practice Part 1: See Yourself Reflected Back to You

This month's practice gets you looking at the deeper layers of who you are by understanding how your brain is uniquely wired. Your goal in Part 1 of this month's practice is to read the eight **Cognitive Function descriptions** that follow and discover what you resonate with the most – **where do you see pieces of yourself reflected back to you?**

Some helpful things to consider as you're reading through the descriptions...

The Driver Function

These eight mental processes, or cognitive functions, that you will read about below, exist in various orders as a "stack" for each one of us, from strongest to weakest. So, it's likely you'll see bits and pieces of yourself in many of the descriptions as we all have access to at least some aspect of each of these eight processes.

But there is one main process that truly drives us and gives us energy – in fact, it's often referred to as "the Driver" – and it's the process that essentially recharges our batteries when we use it.[25] Even when we're actively trying to use other mental processes, there's something about this particular process that still finds a way to show up, and tends to flavor everything we do. Although the end goal is eventually developing a working relationship with all of these parts of ourselves, suffice to say that no matter what adventures we take ourselves on, our Driver function is always there driving the car.

See if you can discover your own Driver process in the following eight descriptions – the one process that really speaks to you, and describes the way you are when you're allowed to be at your most natural state without having to fit in or put on a mask. When you're using this process, it tends to feels like a flow state, and it's easy to lose track of time. It's the place that doesn't drain you at all to be there; it actually gives you energy when you act in this way and you feel like you could do it forever.

While your Driver process is the one that *likely* comes the most naturally and gives you the most energy, it is possible to have a conflicted relationship with it. How we were raised, family values, unhelpful gender stereotypes like the outdated belief that men should be thinkers and women should be feelers, societal expectations like the *Extrovert Ideal* or the undervaluing of intuitive processes, for example – all contribute to whether or not your Driver function is currently operating as your strongest process. Which is why it's so important to discover this information about ourselves, remove any blocks and limiting beliefs, and allow ourselves to access one of our greatest sources of energy.

The Balancing Function

You may find that you resonate strongly with one extraverted process and one introverted process, as we all have both of these sides as explained above in the "Ambivert" section. While our Driver process is the one that we tend to prefer, since it gives us the most energy, our secondary process is the balancing force. This is also a place of great natural talent. This talent may be tapped or untapped at the moment, as sometimes we must exercise a bit of effort to use this secondary balancing process. But it's a process that offers great reward in our lives and contributes an important aspect to our unique style of genius. In the "Car Model" of personality type as posited by Joel Mark Witt and Antonia Dodge, this secondary process is called the "Co-Pilot" and offers great support to the primary "Driver" function.[26]

Cognitive Functions and Myers Briggs

These cognitive functions discovered by Carl Jung are actually the building blocks of the more familiar Myers Briggs theory of personality type. In the 1940s, mother-daughter duo Katherine Briggs and Isabel Briggs Myers created an assessment meant to quickly measure the first and second cognitive functions a person was wired to use, creating 16 types. Over the years, however, much of the nuance of this system has been lost to the general public, as the focus has moved away from the cognitive functions and become entirely on the "either-or" dichotomies of introversion vs. extraversion (I/E), sensing vs. intuiting (S/N), thinking vs. feeling (T/F), and judging vs. perceiving (J/P). With the advent of the internet and the many online quizzes that now exist to determine your personality type, even more nuance has been lost to overly stereotypical descriptions of each of the types.

One criticism of the Myers Briggs system is often how saccharine and over-the-top positive the type descriptions can be. This makes sense because our top two mental processes are inherently places of natural talent for us, and if we only focus on our strengths, we're going to sound amazing. But with every light there is a shadow. No matter how brightly we shine using our first and second cognitive functions, there are always going to be inherent blind spots. In the descriptions that follow you'll read about each cognitive function's natural gifts, talents and strengths, as well as the ways that each function struggles in the world and how it tends to trip us up. It can be healing to simply see and understand our blind spots; we can use that information to stop forcing ourselves to act in ways that are completely unnatural for us and perhaps a little soul-sucking. Over time, we can also choose to see our blind spots as opportunities for personal growth, balance, and the creation of cognitive wholeness.

A Note Regarding Online Quizzes

While there are many Myers Briggs quizzes offered online, as mentioned, they often do not provide accurate results or take much nuance into account, and they typically do not go deep enough, or at all, into the cognitive functions to provide much value. While they are fun, I don't recommend these resources as a reliable source of self-discovery. In general, if a Myers Briggs assessment or type description does not mention the term "cognitive function," I would steer clear of putting much stock in it, as you will lose much of the value, accuracy and depth. There are also the limitations of forced-choice questions. Quizzes typically force us to choose one way that we usually behave – but what if you have a "work self," a "home self," and a "parent self" that are all just a little bit different? The more accurate response to questions about our behavior much of the time is, *"it depends."* But most quizzes are not equipped to take this kind of nuance into account.

And then there's the issue of measuring our external *behaviors,* rather than our internal *motivations* driven by our brain wiring. In the end, we are less interested in all the ways that we *can* behave – all the hats that we can wear when necessary – and more interested in getting at the "who" we are underneath all of that. How is your brain actually wired? But this is again hard to assess in a quiz because it is based on self-assessment. Quizzes ask us to objectively assess ourselves without bias. While developing self-awareness is a natural part of the journey of personal discovery and growth work, we often don't begin with a very accurate picture of who we are, and often fail to objectively assess ourselves with much accuracy. In the end, the quiz may just tell us how we choose to see ourselves, or how the world has told us to see ourselves, but not as who and how we truly are. So, don't worry if you struggle to determine your Driver process right off the bat, even as you read the type descriptions below – I struggled with that, too, at the beginning! Just know that as you continue to develop self-awareness and keep a curious and open mindset, the type will begin to reveal itself to you.

To Learn More

Remember that the following information is just one important piece of understanding how we are uniquely wired to move through the world. If you're curious to learn more about this fascinating system, I recommend checking out the *Personality Hacker* book, or podcast of the same name, with Joel Mark Witt and Antonia Dodge, which are both rich with in-depth information that is easy to understand, or exploring Dr. Dario Nardi's work with personality type from a neuroscience perspective.[27] There are other good sources out there, but I can vouch for both of these being extremely accessible as well as reliable. I also offer a limited number of one-on-one personality profiling sessions in the format of an interview to help you discover your best fit type, if you get stuck on your own or want to dive even deeper.

Recognizing Ourselves - and Others

So, explore the following eight cognitive function descriptions and notice where you see parts of yourself reflected back to you – both your strengths, as well as those areas that tend to trip you up again and again. I wrote the descriptions in a way that I hope will be easy to recognize yourself in them – and to compare and contrast with the other processes in order to rule out those that are not your strongest functions. Keep in mind that these are descriptions of mental processes and the most common ways that they manifest in a person – but each individual human being has a lot of nuance that goes into who and how they are, so a process might look slightly different in one person versus another.

You will probably recognize other people you know reflected in some of the descriptions as well, which is wonderful because this can also be an amazing tool for more deeply understanding the quirks, frustrations and gifts of those we are in relationship with – partners, parents, siblings, children, friends, coworkers, and bosses to name a few. Each description also contains a brief section on the "hidden personality," or those ways we occasionally behave that seem quite unlike us, typically triggered by being under immense stress.[28] In fact, you might find it easier to see those qualities in other people more so than in yourself, because sometimes we turn a blind eye to our deepest blind spots.

So, read on with a curious and reflective mindset and enjoy the process of self-discovery!

Question: Which of the following eight processes describes me the most?

Descriptions for the 8 Cognitive Functions:

The 4 Kinds of Extraversion:

1. Extraverted Feeling (abbreviated Fe)

"Harmonizing & Connecting Energy / Social Butterfly"

The "Driver" process of Myers Briggs types: ESFJ and ENFJ

(The Balancing Function of types: ISFJ and INFJ)

This is the more stereotypical social butterfly, the kind of extraversion that I think we are most familiar with. These folks tend to be the ones who love parties and people and will go to great lengths to do just about anything for you. They are tuned less into the experience of their own inner world of feelings, and more into the feelings that exist externally between people, giving them a keen interest in relationships and interpersonal dynamics.

They will often find themselves in human-centric leadership positions because they can so naturally see how to meet the needs of individuals and groups, and tend to have a knack for mentoring and supporting others. They are often stereotypically found in customer service, sales, human resources, management or counseling roles – anything that allows them to focus on the elements of human connection, persuasion, or enthusiastic encouragement.

They can create rapport very quickly and likely have an easy time making friends, possibly due to their propensity for smiling broadly and asking you lots of questions. They likely exude a warm, cheerful vibe and there's a good chance they use a lot of exclamation points to communicate their thrill of communicating with you!!

They want to create an emotional connection, so will put a lot of their emotions on the outside, hoping to spark that same reciprocity in others. However, they won't often share vulnerably as their focus can be on keeping everyone "feeling good." Other types may see this as inauthentic, but they see it as choosing to focus on what is positive and socially acceptable.

They can read a room and gauge someone's emotional response very quickly, so their communication can often be more passive, almost indirect, as they will do everything they can to avoid intentionally stepping on someone's toes or hurting someone's feelings. Because they can feel the emotions around them so easily, they usually avoid creating awkward situations for themselves or others, because they will be the ones to feel the discomfort the most deeply.

When under the grip of stress, or when not at a healthy level of development, these are ironically the ones that can become the "mean girls" or "mean guys" and become overly tuned into social hierarchy and status, or even say uncharacteristically catty or judgmental things – towards themselves or others.

They tend to struggle with any system relying exclusively on logical reasoning abilities such as mathematics, as well as the ability to clearly articulate their point of view despite feeling very emotionally passionate about something. They can also struggle with having such a natural focus on others that it can make it hard for them to self-reflect or develop deep self-awareness. Or they may wake up one day to discover that all of their relationships and friendships are one-sided, as they have given up their own authenticity in favor of people-pleasing, not speaking their truth, and always being the helper there for everyone else's needs except their own.

What this mental process asks is: *How can I create a connection with another individual? How can I be a positive and contributing member of the group? Does this meet everyone's needs?*

2. Extraverted Thinking (abbreviated Te)

"Doing Energy – to get it done / Strategist"

The "Driver" process of Myers Briggs types: ESTJ and ENTJ

(The Balancing Function of types: ISTJ and INTJ)

Then there's the extraverts that don't necessarily need the social stimulation, but are the classic *do-ers* of the world and derive great pleasure from *getting shit done* – effectively and quickly.

They don't need to know every single piece of information available – in fact that will likely exasperate them – as they want to get from point A to B! They are interested in the data points around them so long as they are deemed applicable, which means they are useful in moving them closer to meeting their goal. They are extremely goal-oriented and naturally talented at marshalling resources towards that goal, whether those resources are human or material. They love to strategize the best course of action, and then implement that plan in a very linear, step-by-step fashion.

They are the stereotypical managers, executives, and entrepreneurs of the world and often find themselves in a natural leadership role – of their work team, their family, their friends, heading an entire organization, or whatever group they find themselves a part of. If no one else is stepping up into a position of leadership, they will sometimes become reluctant leaders even when they don't want to in a particular situation, simply because they can so easily see what needs to happen and how to organize the chaos.

They will naturally create processes, procedures and rules, and are gifted at establishing, streamlining, and scaling up systems to amplify their impact with less input. They are known for being extremely organized and timely. Punctuality likely comes easily to them, and it will be expected of you, as well.

Communication wise, they will likely prefer to keep their feelings more internal, and communicate in the most efficient way possible to get straight to the point. They are often more assertive and direct, and when it comes to using punctuation in written communication, have a reputation for preferring the straightforward period over feelings-laden exclamation points. While their style of communication can sometimes be perceived as cold or curt, to them it's just quick and efficient.

When under the grip of stress, or when not at a healthy level of development, they may bulldoze other's ideas or feelings, seeing their plan as the only permissible course of action. So driven to achieve a goal, they may not take the time to first align with their values or ethics and wake up one day to find themselves chasing after a goal that isn't that personally important to them, or pursuing a goal that is somewhat destructive.

Endless do-ers, they tend to struggle with just "being" or enjoying slowness or stillness. Due to this, they may have workaholic tendencies, or struggle with taking the time to appreciate the more intangible, qualitative aspects of life like beauty, art, and human emotion. When faced with intense emotional situations, they may feel quite panicked and overwhelmed about how to process their deep feelings. Emotions can be a challenge for these types; they typically dislike the idea of being vulnerable or showing their soft underbelly, and knowing what they are feeling – and why they are feeling that way – in any given moment can be an ongoing challenge for them.

What this mental process asks is: *How do we get effectively from point A to B? How can I strategize the best course of action or have the most impact? Does this work?*

3. Extraverted Sensing (abbreviated Se)

"Action Energy – for the pure thrill of it / Adventurer"

The "Driver" process of Myers Briggs types: ESFP and ESTP

(The Balancing Function of types: ISFP and ISTP)

Then there are the extraverts who get their energy from kinesthetic/aesthetic/physical enjoyment, who tend to prioritize and enjoy experiences using their five senses and their bodies.

Their goal is less about the accomplishment of getting things done – they likely don't make or follow organized to-do lists – but they love to get into action and experience the thrill of being alive. They are known for having a lot of charisma, are typically comfortable being the center of attention, and may find that others are often drawn to them for the energy, spontaneity, and adventure they bring to whatever they undertake.

They are focused on real-time, in-the-moment experiences, and are very quick to respond to information coming at them in the sensory world. Because of this, they are often the stereotypical athletes and first-responders of the world, as well as the adrenaline junkies and the explorers who are always up for a new adventure.

Craving an intensity of sensory experience, they may view the world through a lens of, *"how much fun can I have right now?"* or *"how can I involve all of my senses in this moment?"* So connected to themselves on a grounded, physical level, these individuals may struggle mentally and emotionally more than other types with an illness or injury that disconnects them from their innate physicality.

They are typically hands-on learners and can have trouble learning if they aren't allowed to physically engage with it themselves. They can likewise feel skeptical or have trouble believing an idea or concept that they have never personally experienced. Simply providing these individuals with the experience is the validation they require. While this doesn't always translate well to the required book-learning of traditional school, they are often the ones that can pick up a tool or instrument and immediately make sense of it, assess a broken item in the house and understand how to fix it, or hop on a stage and spontaneously entertain with confidence.

Communication wise, they likely text in short, fast bursts with little punctuation. Better yet, they'd prefer to hop on the phone or communicate in person – real time communication – so they don't risk completely forgetting to reply to your message.

Usually carefree and grounded in the present moment, when under the grip of stress or when not at a healthy level of development, they may become uncharacteristically stressed about the future and the passage of time, seeing only impending doom as they try to gaze into future possibilities. They may also become paranoid or suspicious, attributing malevolent intentions to others where there are none.

So grounded in their own experience, they tend to struggle with seeing and understanding others' perspectives as this is something that is hard to personally experience at a tangible level. Loving to get into action, they can also struggle with having patience and can be overly impulsive as the time for them is always, *now!* And being so attuned to the present moment, they can have a hard time conceptualizing both past and future, which can at times make it hard to learn from past mistakes, or likewise to fully think through the future consequences of an action.

What this mental process asks is: *How can I feel the most alive? What can I experience right now in the present moment? Can I verify this using my five senses?*

4. Extraverted Intuition (abbreviated Ne)

"Abstract Analyzing Energy / Explorer"

The "Driver" process of Myers Briggs types: ENFP and ENTP

(The Balancing Function of types: INFP and INTP)

And, last but not least, are the more abstract extraverts, the out-of-the-box thinkers, who derive their energy from brainstorming, generating and playing with ideas, and making connections in the outer world in service of learning and seeing the bigger picture.

Similar to all extraverts, these individuals are also tuned into the environment around them, but instead of hyper focusing on one element – feelings, data, or sensations – they tune into the patterns that exist externally. Whereas Extraverted Sensing would hyper focus on the tree in front of them to have the most thrilling experience of that tree, metaphorically speaking, Extraverted Intuition zooms so far out that they can see the entire forest – in order to better see the connections. They see the world as endlessly full of possibilities, and love exploring new ideas and concepts.

They tend to be insatiably curious and radically open-minded, loving to explore the big existential questions about the nature of reality. Delighted by new information, they enjoy anything that allows them to endlessly broaden their understanding of what it all means.

They are the stereotypical detectives, inventors, and provocateurs of the world – connecting the seemingly disparate clues, envisioning what has never before existed, and poking at the established system in order to make it better – or often to their delight, to rip it down entirely. In a tangible sense they are often found in creative or visionary positions – starting a new company, carrying the vision for a group, or engaged in consulting or creative directing roles.

Loving possibilities and with an immense amount of energy for the start-up phase of any project, they may often find themselves ridings waves of chaos as they excitedly take on huge workloads or begin nine projects at once, only to then realize their human limits.

Their communication style is likely a combination of deep analysis of the world around them, and absurd witty banter.

Due to this outside-the-box mentality about life, these extraverts often feel somewhat misunderstood as their particular brand of extraversion doesn't always fit the societal mold. At the same time, being extraverts, they report having a hard time keeping their unique and revolutionary ideas to themselves, and for better and for worse, find themselves taking on the role of the class clown, the misfit, the weird kid – until they can come to appreciate their gifts and feel empowered to help improve the world around them.

When under the grip of stress, or when not at a healthy level of development, they may become uncharacteristically stressed about "following the rules," something they are typically unconcerned about. This is usually triggered by a situation where there is very little room for creativity or error, and requires intense attention to detail, like filing taxes or filling out important forms. Usually hopeful, they can also become quite fatalistic when deeply stressed, certain that their current unpleasant situation will never end.

They tend to struggle with anything that requires ongoing maintenance or consistency across time – habits, routines, schedules – and can completely lose their energetic spark when it comes to finishing the last twenty-percent or so of a project. They can struggle with commitment, suffer from a lack of groundedness – feeling at odds with anything too "sensible" or "practical" – and often appear to exist in a realm of total disconnection from time.

What this mental process asks is: *How can I connect these seemingly unconnected points? What can I do or create that has never been done before? Can I improve upon or expand this idea or system? What if...(fill in the blank)?*

The Four Kinds of Introversion:

1. Introverted Feeling (abbreviated Fi)

"Inner Feelings Energy / Inspirer"

The "Driver" process of Myers Briggs types: ISFP and INFP

(The Balancing Function of types: ESFP and ENFP)

Though another feeling process, Introverted Feeling can look extremely different from Extraverted Feeling as this is less about the exchange of feelings between individuals, and more about the individual's experience of their own deep inner world of feelings.

Experiencing intense, nuanced, and far-ranging emotions, these introverts tend to be driven by self-expression, seeking a way to share this complex inner world of feelings that can't be captured by mere language. They are therefore often the stereotypical artists of the world, using mediums such as song, dance, art, poetry, fashion, etc. to convey these feelings in the tangible, material world.

Deeply tied to their personal values and ethics, Introverted Feeling users tend to be very introspective, reflective, and quietly inspirational by so deeply embodying their beliefs. Valuing authenticity above all else, these individuals allow space for everyone to be exactly that – their own unique individual. Having little interest in conformity, they are driven not by societal expectations, but by personal feelings. What they present to the world on the outside will be a reflection of their inner experience. And they will be the most accepting of your own decision to express yourself in whatever way is most authentic to you.

Despite this extremely layered and complex emotional experience occurring inside these individuals, they may seem rather stoic or reserved – even more so in males due to the outdated gender stereotype that men shouldn't show their emotions. Contrasted with the more exuberant Extraverted Feeling types, it may even be hard to initially pinpoint these types as "feeling" types at all. But if you take the time to really go deep with these individuals, you may find that they can naturally create a comfort of vulnerable emotionality that typically cannot be experienced in our fast-paced, surface small talk.

Usually gentle and sensitive beings, when under the grip of stress, or when not at a healthy level of development, they can become uncharacteristically demanding, aggressive, controlling, or selfish. They may explode in anger, make rash decisions, or suddenly attempt to lay down outrageous rules in order to feel that they have some control of the situation.

They tend to struggle with having to do anything they are not feeling personally motivated to do. Being so tied to what they are feeling in each moment, they can find it hard to make plans as it's impossible to predict how one will feel in the future – or to stick to those plans if the mood changes. It can be quite a challenge for them to compartmentalize feelings to deal with later, or to rally to a situation despite what they might be feeling internally. Extremely inner directed, it can be hard for them to do something that a group has decided to do if it doesn't match with what they personally feel like doing. They may find it hard or draining to manage people or resources, easily tire of constant external communication, and feel tentative about giving advice or stepping up into positions of leadership.

What this mental process asks is: *Does this feel right to me? What is my emotional experience of this? Is this in alignment with my values?*

2. Introverted Thinking (abbreviated Ti)

"Logical Reasoning Energy / Rationalist"

The "Driver" process of Myers Briggs types: ISTP and INTP

(The Balancing Function of types: ESTP and ENTP)

Though another thinking process, Introverted Thinking can look extremely different from Extraverted Thinking as this is less about quickly and efficiently getting from point A to B, and more about a collection of all of the information available. Whereas Extraverted Thinking individuals would often become exasperated with too much information that just slows down a decision, Introverted Thinking focuses on accuracy, and these individuals will not make their decision until they have deemed that all of the information available and relevant to the decision has first been considered.

Because there can often be too much data to consider all at once, these individuals excel at creating frameworks as a way to organize a part of the data. They are therefore often the stereotypical scientists and mathematicians of the world, able to consider vast amounts of complicated data – especially numerical – and organize and simplify it via complex systems and processes. They are also often the stereotypical mechanics, machinists, and surgeons, able to naturally understand and master any kind of system or machine, whether human or mechanical.

These individuals value truth, accuracy and congruity with a focus on clean, clear, objective and rational thought. You won't find them blindly following societal expectations unless these make sense on a personal level to the Introverted Thinking user. Tied primarily to their own internal standards, they will easily question authority placing truth and correctness above external factors like social hierarchy, status or authority. Valuing marching to the beat of what makes sense to their own inner logic, they may likewise find themselves at odds with social niceties and norms, and stand out in ways that make them somewhat of the social outcast as the stereotypical nerd, geek, rebel, or even outlaw.

Because they have an extreme focus on accuracy, they typically also have a close relationship with radical honesty, being compelled to provide the truthful information rather than the socially acceptable information. Whereas other individuals using other mental processes may err on the side of saying the nice thing instead of the truthful thing – which has its own downfalls – the Introverted Thinking individual has likely had the experience of being called "tactless" as they navigate the fine line between honesty and kindness. On the flip side, they've likely also had the experience of being called funny or humorous, as the best comedy typically has a grain of hard, honest truth to it.

Usually cool and logical, when under the grip of stress, or when not at a healthy level of development, they may uncharacteristically explode in a tantrum of feelings. Typically easygoing and mentally sharp, they may become extremely demanding or illogical, or even reject new information that threatens to corrupt a framework they have spent much time perfecting. While often quite loyal to those they make connections with, they may actually stay in unhealthy relationships out of the fear of finding anyone else to connect with.

They tend to struggle with anything that defies logic, including their own and other's emotions. While these individuals are often extremely intellectually bright and intelligent, they may find that emotional and relational intelligence is more of a mystery. Knowing what they feel in any given moment can be an ongoing challenge, as well as navigating the often-messy dynamics of interpersonal relationships. They still crave that feeling of connection we all long for, but often feel perplexed at how to create such a connection or express what they are feeling to others. Likewise, since social expectations often defy any set of logical rules, they can struggle with wanting to follow this agreed upon collection of niceties and norms, not understanding how this creates disconnection from others.

What this mental process asks is: *Does this make sense to me? Is this logical? Do I need more data to think more clearly about this?*

3. Introverted Sensing (abbreviated Si)

"Concrete Learning & Maintenance Energy / Legacy Keeper"

The "Driver" process of Myers Briggs types: ISFJ and ISTJ

(The Balancing Function of types: ESFJ and ESTJ)

Though another sensing process, Introverted Sensing can look quite different from Extraverted Sensing as the focus is less about real-time, in the moment, heightened experiences of aliveness, and more about collecting experiences for the sake of learning.

While both enjoy partaking in sensory experiences, Extraverted Sensing individuals tend to have a more cavalier, devil-may-care approach to life, whereas Introverted Sensing folks prefer their experiences bolstered with a sense of reliability, safety, and predictability. More than anyone else, they tend to enjoy their routines and returning to the same places again and again in order to revisit their favorite past experiences and memories.

They tend to be responsible and consistent individuals who live their lives in a grounded, practical way. Because of their conscientiousness and valuing of standards and structures, they are often the stereotypical "good citizens," who mow their pristine lawns regularly, always turn out to vote, and pay their taxes on time. Because of this attunement to the structures of society, and their natural ability to be relied upon, they may find themselves involved in local or national government, or working as part of the institutions that ground and stabilize our culture like banks, schools, and religious establishments.

The stereotypical administrator of any organization, these individuals excel at tasks involving organization, implementation, and the attention to detail that is vital for keeping operations running smoothly. They may find they are just as likely to play this role in a professional capacity, as well as for their own family.

Because of their proclivity to revisit an experience again and again, they are also the stereotypical specialists, able to develop a highly nuanced expertise in a field. After experiencing something again and again, they often show up with a very specific idea of how something should go – they are the most likely to want to carry on traditions in the exact fashion they've always been carried on, adhere to established rules, and tend to feel most comfortable relying upon the tried-and-true method.

At the same time, when encountering something brand new without a framework to fit it into, they may feel a little skeptical or overwhelmed at first – new information might strike this function as unwelcome when compared against what it already knows and understands. But, if the Introverted Sensing user sticks with it over time, they will find their brains have an immense ability to adapt to new information and new situations.

Typically stable and reliable, when under the grip of stress, or when not at a healthy level of development, they may make uncharacteristically impulsive and rash decisions when their tried-and-true methods aren't solving the problem at hand. They may also find they become expert catastrophizers, coming up with all sorts of creative, horrible, but totally unwarranted, possibilities about what's really happening in a stressful situation, or perhaps slide all the way into ongoing negativity and pessimism about life in general.

They tend to struggle with "outside-the-box" thinking, questioning authority, or the open-minded exploration of new ideas and concepts. Naturally attuned to the past, they may find it easy to get stuck there, unable to envision new future possibilities, and can struggle with taking the risks needed to expand their horizons and grow.

What this mental process asks is: *Is this reliable and safe? Can I verify this against what is known? How can I revisit my favorite past experiences and memories? What practical skills could I master?*

4. Introverted Intuition (abbreviated Ni)

"Abstract Learning Energy / Visionary"

The "Driver" process of Myers Briggs types: INFJ and INTJ

(The Balancing Function of types: ENFJ and ENTJ)

Though another intuiting process, Introverted Intuition can look quite different from Extraverted Intuition with less of a focus on external, real-time pattern-recognition, and more of a focus on internal patterns of consciousness, as well as future prediction. Similar to Extraverted Intuition though, Introverted Intuition, too, will zoom out far enough to see the entire forest, metaphorically speaking. But while the Extraverted Intuition individual will be able to tap into a real-time experience of the unique connections possible between disparate trees of the forest, the Introverted Intuition individual's magic will happen later, after they've exited the forest and continue to ponder the questions this experience has presented such as, *what is the meaning of this forest? What even is a forest? What can this forest teach us? If we continue on in this way, what will this forest look like in the future?*

Similar to all introverts, individuals using Introverted Intuition turn their attention inward to their inner world, but instead of hyper focusing on their own feelings, thoughts, or experiences and memories like the other introverted processes, their attention is directed more to the realm of their ideas.

Instead of the "outside-the-box" thinking often ascribed to Extraverted Intuition, Introverted Intuition users tend to think *about* the box itself. The questions they ponder often begin with their favorite word, *"Why?"* Taking almost nothing for granted, they seem to wonder – why is anything the way it is? By getting to the root of things, holding space for nuance, complexity and paradox, and aiming to conceptually understand the meaning of everything, the Introverted Intuition user attempts to gather an understanding of the very nature of reality itself.

By subconsciously understanding how their own mind works, individuals using Introverted Intuition also tend to have a knack for getting inside the minds of others. Because of this, they are able to quickly switch perspectives from their own into another's, and readily put themselves into other people's shoes. Finding it so easy and natural to quickly switch perspectives, they may find they have a hard time sticking to their own perspective – or even feeling clear on what that is. Having an ability to float between perspectives, they make natural mediators and may find they are quick to assist others in disagreements or misunderstandings as they can easily fill in the gaps and provide the bridge in understanding between two opposing individuals or groups.

Having a keen ability to see and extrapolate patterns – into other's minds, between two opposing sides, as well as into the future – along with a close relationship to imagination and a propensity for deep contemplation, they are often the stereotypical philosophers, psychologists, and spiritual teachers, as well as futurists, prophets, and seers, providing vision, warning, and hope of what's to come.

Though their minds are endlessly busy, they may physically appear quiet, reserved, almost motionless. But their still waters run deep, and if you take the time to slow down and deeply listen to them, you may discover a mad array of fascinating questions about the world and thoughtful observations about yourself that we typically do not have access to in our surface, fast paced world.

When under the grip of stress, or when not at a healthy level of development, they can find themselves overdoing sensory pleasures such as overeating, overindulging in sweets, drinking too much, or becoming overly-focused on physical pursuits like exercising to excess or hyper-controlling their diet to deal with health issues. So astute at synthesizing complex information within their minds, they may experience a child-like overwhelm or panic with complex – or even basic – sensory situations in the external world, like operating a new vehicle with all its tools and gadgets or navigating a foreign city.

So prone to contemplation, they tend to struggle with the ability to jump into action or make a quick decision. Typically a bit disconnected from their physicality and sensory surroundings, they may struggle with clumsiness, physical coordination, or the simple task of walking through a room without stubbing their toes. Often already living in their mind lightyears into the future, they may find it a challenge to execute all the tangible steps needed to get from step one to step fifty in order to carry out the vision they so clearly see, feeling frustrated that it's not coming into fruition.

What this mental process asks is: *What is the deeper meaning of this? What is really going on here below the surface? How can I translate this? What is my vision for the future? Why...(fill in the blank)?*

Practice Part 2: Journal/Reflect

Now that you've read the 8 descriptions above and are probably starting to see pieces of yourself within them, I recommend you get out your journal and allow yourself to reflect on the following questions:

1. **Of the 4 <u>extraverted</u> descriptions, which one sounds the most like me?** It's ok if you see elements of yourself in more than one process; see if you can intuitively choose one for now.
   - Write down the aspects of this process that you see in yourself.

- Ask yourself, do these characteristics make me feel in alignment with society's expectations of how we are "supposed to be" or different from society? In what ways?
- How does that make me feel?

2. **Of the 4 <u>introverted</u> descriptions, which one sounds the most like me?** Again, it's ok to see yourself in more than one process; see if you can intuitively choose one for now.
    - Write down the aspects of this process that you see in yourself.
    - Ask yourself, do these characteristics make me feel in alignment with society's expectations of how we are "supposed to be" or different from society? In what ways?
    - How does that make me feel?

3. **What do I truly love to do?** Those moments when I realize three hours have passed and I've forgotten to pee or eat because I'm so engaged in whatever is happening – what am I doing? Remember, this thing (or things) we so deeply love to do is typically directly connected to our Driver process, and recharges and re-energizes us, just like plugging in our phone battery when it's waning. It's not always a nap that we need when we're feeling low; oftentimes it's needing to give ourselves the time and space to engage in this thing we love to do.
    - Write down everything about this state – where you typically are, who you're usually with (or are you usually alone?), and what you're typically engaging in.

- How often do I allow myself to engage in this thing that I truly love to do? Is it a regular occurrence or something I rarely get to enjoy?
- If it's rare, how can I commit to creating the space to do that more often this month?

Practice Part 3: Make a Commitment

Now, make a commitment to two things this month:

1. Commit to giving yourself permission to be more of who and how you are, even if that differs from society's expectations of how we are "supposed to be." Write in your journal or state out loud:

    I commit to giving myself permission to be more of who and how I am, even if that differs from society's expectations of how we are "supposed to be!"

Then decide on one concrete way you can do that this month. Maybe it's repeating the above affirmation daily, or taking a particular action like saying no to something that drains you or saying yes to something that lights you up, etc. There are no wrong answers, choose whatever feels right to you. Write it down so that you can remind yourself about this commitment throughout the month. Keep this written commitment somewhere you can see daily, like on a closet or a mirror.

2. Commit to creating the space to do more of the activities you love to do – the things that light you up and give you energy. Write in your journal or state out loud:

I commit to creating the space to do more of the activities I love to do, the things that light me up, and give me energy!

Then decide on one concrete way you can do that this month. Maybe it's creating a weekly space in your calendar to engage in the thing you love to do – which might require letting go of a different commitment that feels heavy so you can replace it with the thing you actually do love to do. Or maybe the white space you create in your calendar IS the thing you love to do – making time for the conscious act of doing nothing. Reach out to a friend so you can make a date to do this thing out in the world together. Or, rain-check a plan with a friend so you can make a date with *yourself* to do this thing you love to do, alone! Again, there are no wrong answers, write down here whatever feels right to you. I recommend writing it down *and* putting it in your calendar so you can remind yourself about this commitment throughout this month!

Journey Onward

Some of the most important questions we can ask ourselves are: *Who am I? Why am I here? How can I heal and grow?* My journey is to answer these questions for myself, as well as to guide others in finding their own answers.

At this point on my journey, I love knowing deeply who I am, and I continue to enjoy the journey of discovering ever deepening layers. I am coming to understand more clearly and succinctly my purpose at its core, although it can take many manifestations of what this looks like! And I am in the ongoing process of shedding what is not me, in the process of the deep work of healing and growing, the process of re-embodying what I once was but in a way that is even more vibrant and whole than ever before. Where are YOU on your journey of answering these questions?

May you enjoy this journey of self-discovery! And Happy Leo season, friends! May you feel an extra boost of confidence over the next month to embody and express the true personality of your soul. May you experience the joy, freedom and fulfillment that comes with living a life aligned with your authentic self. And in so doing, may all your cells align in health.

CHAPTER 6

August:
Slowing Down Time

EVERY YEAR AS THE SUMMER begins to wane, we look back and think, *how time flies!* Desperate to get the most out of the remaining season, we do more and more, filling our schedules to the brim with the last kernels of summertime – sure that *doing* is the secret to mastering time once and for all. It does make some sense – if we fill our time, we're always making the most of it, right? Always one step ahead of the sneaky time devil, never in danger of wasting any time at all. We tend to operate this way not only in the sweet last remaining days of summer, but pretty much – well, all the time. But if our time is always so beautifully full and abundant, then *why* does it still always feel like time is flying by??

"*Time flies*" is one of those common sayings we've uttered so many times we barely give it a second thought. Catchy sayings about time abound in our culture: *Time waits for no one. Don't waste time! I'm trying to save time. I'm just killing time. We're in a race against time! We have all the time in the world. Time is money. Spend your time wisely. Lost time is never found again. Time is slipping away.*

You've heard these before, I'm sure! These phrases say a lot about the very nature of our relationship with time. A relationship that is based on scarcity, with a thief who takes from us. Believing that time is a limited resource we convince ourselves that we must control it, master it, locking ourselves into an endless battle against a force that won't stop marching ever forward.

In Time Lives Our Greatest Fear

Our struggle can feel fruitless. So, we laugh, throw our hands up in the air and say, *there's just never enough time!* You either laugh or you cry – because in time lives also our greatest fear. That one day our time will finally run out, our ticker will finally stop ticking, and other time related sayings about our personal end of days.

Time has become a commodity as valuable to us as money, but one we try in vain to save. Despite our best efforts to stockpile time, in the end, everyone is given the same amount of time – in a day, in a week, in a year. But perhaps what keeps us so gripped by time is the one unknown when it comes to this usually measurable resource – how much of it we have in a lifetime. Which puts us face to face with the one question we never want to acknowledge, and the one answer we never want to face. That we don't know how much time we have on this Earth, but we do know that one day we will be gone.

It's the great question – if you knew that today was your last day on this Earth, what would you do? Would you live your life differently if you knew you had exactly one month, or one year, or one hundred years left to live? Not knowing, we exist somewhere between believing that time is endless, and feeling terrified that we'll run out too soon.

Though we try our best to manage time, it seems that time is actually the ultimate controller, pulling the strings of our lives. But do you want to know a secret? There is an art to mastering time, to ending the great race. And it doesn't have anything to do with doing more; in fact, it's quite the opposite.

Kairos Time and Chronos Time

So how do we change our relationship with time? Our most common sayings about time are speaking to our relationship with Father Time, also known as *"Chronos time."* Chronos is one of two Greek words meaning "time." It's also the root of the words *"chronicle"* and *"chronological."* Chronos time is the measurable, quantifiable aspect of time. It is linear time – recorded by calendars to measure a year, by clocks to measure a day. It is the more masculine/yang aspect of time. It is based on external measurements rather than internal feelings and sensations.

Tied only to Chronos time, we may go to bed at a certain time not because we feel tired, but because it is our bedtime. We may wake up by an alarm clock that cares little that we desperately desire more sleep. We may eat at prescribed hours because those are the agreed upon hours that a person should eat. We may go to our job for eight hours not because we always have eight hours worth of work, but because we are getting paid to be there for eight hours. And we may spend forty hours there each week not because that feels right in our soul, but because someone decided that forty hours was the correct measurement of a workweek.

Living our lives by Chronos time alone, we may find that nearly every moment of our lives is tied to something happening at the "right" time on the clock. That we're scheduled so tightly we barely have room to breathe, let alone think or truly feel about what's on our insides.

But unlike us, the Greeks also had a second word for the concept of time: "Kairos." Whereas Chronos time is the measurable, quantifiable aspect of time, Kairos time is the immeasurable, qualitative aspect of time. It is the more feminine/yin aspect of time. It expands and deepens our perception of time. It is time that seems to exist outside of time, and also deep inside of time. As Robert Moss describes in his book *Sidewalk Oracles: Playing with Signs, Symbols, and Synchronicity in Everyday Life:*

> "Kairos time is when you are released, if only for a moment, from the breakable laws of linear time and space, when things come to you, and you to them, by a different logic."[29]

It's those moments when we feel forces beyond chance at play – when a mere coincidence becomes a meaningful synchronicity, and a synchronicity becomes a divine orchestration. Kairos moments have a sacred, spiritual, otherworldly quality to them. They are moments when we feel truly connected to ourselves, to nature, to community, to the divine. Sometimes we can access these moments in meditation, and sometimes these moments come and find us in our daily lives.

It's those moments when time literally seems to stand still. Locking eyes for the first time with your future lover and feeling time slow down for an instant. Meeting a kindred spirit for the first time and having that nagging feeling that you somehow already know each other. The job opportunity of a lifetime that comes so wildly out of the blue and gives you the distinct perception of standing at a very important crossroads in your life.

It is also the simplest of moments of holy perfection when we feel connected to our inner self, to a sense of flow, to a nourishing slowness – stopping to truly take in a sunset, gazing at the stars and suddenly understanding your place in the universe, sipping your morning coffee or tea and feeling like everything is going to be ok.

Sometimes it's the feeling that time has sped up. Think of how slowly time seems to move when you're bored; but think of how quickly it seems to fly by when you're deeply engaged in something you love. Those times when you're so immersed you completely forget to look at your watch at all. You swear it's only been twenty minutes, but somehow three hours have passed.

Kairos time can also be a moment of action – when we're fully tuned into the present moment in order to both notice and jump on a perfectly timed opportunity that presents itself and seems almost too good to be true. That feeling of being in the right place at the right time, the happy serendipitous coincidence, the moment of opportunity that feels like it could change your life.

Kairos Time and Creative Pursuits

Kairos time invites us to re-imagine the definition of the *"right"* time. Instead of being exclusively bound by the external measurements of time – *"because it's 4pm, because it's Tuesday"* – we allow ourselves to be open also to internal markers of right timing – *"because it feels right, because I'm inspired."* This idea of paying attention to internal markers of right timing is especially important for creative pursuits. I don't think that anyone suffers from a lack of creativity, but more so a lack of knowing how to create the right conditions to capture our inspiration.

Tuning into Kairos time allows us to seize a burst of inspiration, where we find we produce a higher quality of work with much less effort than we do by trying to force it. This idea has completely changed my relationship to the creative process of writing, for example – a process I used to find extremely stressful. In my wellness coaching business, I send out a newsletter that is less of a "quick updates" endeavor and more of a deep commentary on life in the form of a long essay. But I used to schedule "write newsletter" on my calendar at various times of the month, and have it looming over me until the time when I would sit down at my laptop and proceed to procrastinate for five hours because I had no idea what to write about. Not only was I not making any space to capture the natural moments of inspiration, I was always in a race against time because I typically only gave myself one day to do the whole damn thing!

Tuning in to how I really felt inside and the ways I know my mind naturally works, I started to slow down the whole process, only writing one newsletter per month, and stretching out the process over the course of a few days. In addition to keeping copious notes on any moments of inspiration that would strike earlier in the month, I then gave myself a few hours one day to just allow the space to generate and capture ideas. The next day I carved out a few hours to compose what many writers lovingly refer to as "the shitty first draft." And then another few hours the next day to edit the writing and format the newsletter, etc. And while I would typically send out the newsletter at 8am on a Tuesday morning, I started allowing myself the space to push that Tuesday out by an entire week if life was already getting too busy. Another way of slowing down the race and creating white space.

And surprisingly, two important things started happening. One, the number of newsletter opens nearly doubled. No one was even expecting me to put in as much effort as I was putting in trying to make a twice-monthly newsletter. And two, I started to enjoy writing. It used to be such a stressful process that I dreaded – and fully understood the sentiment of many a writer expressing their joy in *having written*, but loathing the process itself. But now, having integrated Kairos principles into this creative process, it has allowed it to become something that is enjoyable, energizing and peaceful.

Kairos Time All the Time?

Now, it's important to note that I also experimented with swinging the pendulum all the way to the other side and trying to write the newsletter *only* when I felt inspired. Kairos time only, baby!

But I found that without *some* external structure, in the form of loose Chronos deadlines, I wasn't writing at all. I would go months before inspiration struck because I forgot about the importance of intentionally tuning in and paying attention. Without some Kairos time anchored into my Chronos schedule it was too easy to get busy doing other things. You see how they can work together? If we're only valuing one side of a dichotomy it can be destructive, no matter which side. Integrating the two concepts together is really where the magic happens – transforming something stressful or depleting into something that nourishes the soul, *and* making sure that nourishing thing is actually happening!

Maintain Order, Nourish the Soul

We need both Kairos and Chronos time not only in our creative lives, but in order to live in an interdependent society. If everyone acted only and exclusively on their inner feelings and moments of inspiration, it would be chaos. *What time is the meeting? Whenever everyone individually* feels *inspired to show up.* Yeah, that's not going to work! At least not in our culture.

But in our overly-scheduled, calendar-dependent culture, we can use that to our advantage. We can let Chronos and Kairos work together, as they're meant to be. We can use Chronos time to schedule in the Kairos time, just like I did with my writing process. No, we can't schedule when we want a moment of synchronicity – a meaningful coincidence that feels tied to the greater forces of the universe – to occur *for* us, but we can start to create enough white space in our calendar to begin to even be *aware* of them.

We can sometimes be so exclusively tied to Chronos time that we don't allow the spontaneous moments of Kairos time to enter into our awareness. Sometimes a moment of synchronicity, a burst of inspiration, a perfect opportunity may occur and we're too busy to even notice. We just steamroll right on past, onto our next appointment and deadline. We miss not only the big stuff – perhaps orchestrated by the greater forces of the universe itself for our personal benefit, *no big deal* – but the small stuff, too. We miss the gorgeous sunsets, the priceless smiles and snuggles from our children and pups, the deep conversations with kindred spirits – the moments that take us outside of time and remind us that everything is going to be ok.

By scheduling downtime and white space into our calendar, we force ourselves to start to use time in a different way altogether. We allow ourselves the time and space to be open to the Kairos moments that come our way, and we start to actively seek them out as well. And we remind ourselves that of course we need both, – but if Chronos time is what maintains order in our lives, Kairos time is what *nourishes the soul.*

Mother Earth and Father Time

No one can force you to take the time to savor a sunset but you, and it's going to require a temporary stop of "being productive." Lucky for us, this is actually the perfect time of year to support our efforts at slowing down, carving out white space in our calendar, and integrating more Kairos time into our lives.

In Chinese Five Element Theory, there is a fifth season beyond our usual four – the season of Late Summer. The last week of August will usher in this short and sweet month-long season, lasting until the Fall Equinox in mid-September. Though we don't officially have the language or framework for this season in our culture, I think we nonetheless feel it. Sure, externally the weather may continue to look the same as summer, but internally I think we sense a shift afoot. Energetically, this is the shift from yang into yin. And it is a big transition!

The yang energy of Summer is fiery, fast, flickery, expansive, hot, social, passionate, ungrounded. And before this completely gives way to the cool, still, grounded yin energy of Autumn, there is Late Summer – a time of balanced yin and yang. The natural course of fire is to die down eventually. Like a bonfire at the end of the night, the flames return to the earth, settling down into warm glowing embers, before extinguishing completely. This warm, glowing ember stage is the energy of Late Summer. Abundant, but slowing down, releasing heat, turning inward. Rooted, grounded, returning to the Earth.

If our lives are typically bound by the masculine/yang measurements of Father Time, it is Late Summer that perfectly ushers us into the beginning of the feminine/yin cycle, a time when we more naturally feel connected to Mother Earth.

Why Do We Resist It?

As we pay attention to the wisdom of nature and the energy of the seasons that surround us, we may find that it feels more natural to start to slow down and begin to turn inward at this time of year. Or, maybe we tend to feel sadness at the ending of summer. We might feel stuck in this time of transition and not quite ready to let go of the summer and what was. We may resist releasing that comforting feeling of facing outward, of *going going going*, and *doing doing doing*; that fiery masculine/yang energy that we are so culturally accustomed to feeling.

We can ask, why do we resist it? Sure, it might simply be that you dread the physical experience of winter's cold, but I think it's also a great opportunity to dig a little deeper and see what else is there. What is it about slowing down, about turning inwards that makes us uncomfortable? If you notice any resistance or discomfort this time of year as summer begins to give way to autumn, I recommend spending some time exploring the following questions over the next few weeks:

- *Why is it hard for me to welcome in with open arms and joyful heart the season that encourages me to move slower, do less, and self-reflect?*

- *Do I use busyness as a way to avoid looking at certain aspects of myself? Are there parts inside of me that I'm hiding from? What pieces of myself might I be afraid of confronting?*

- *What would have to change in my life in order to slow down? What would have to change in order to do less?*

- *How does the idea of slowing down and doing less make me feel? About myself? About my worth?*

- *Is my worth tied to my productivity? If I am not constantly being productive, do I believe I am not worthwhile?*

- *What moments of Kairos time am I keeping myself from experiencing?*

    o *Am I moving too fast to pause and fully take in a sunset? To truly stop and smell the flowers?*

    o *To breathe deeply enough to feel my breath all the way down into my belly?*

    o *To feel grateful for being here, being alive in this moment?*

    o *To sip my cup of tea or coffee and really taste it, savor it?*

    o *To go so deep into a conversation that I completely lose track of time?*

The Race for...what?

Chronos time marches ever forward, at an anxiety-inducing pace. In the last twenty years of technological advances, it seems to race at a pace we can barely keep up with. One that is making us sick, and unhappy, and oh-so-busy without the time to do what we truly want to do with the time we are given here.

Chronos time isn't bad in and of itself – it serves many helpful functions. But just like any dichotomous idea (*this OR that; Chronos time OR Kairos time*), when left alone without its opposite to balance it, it is destructive. In this time of our lives, as a society we have leaned so far into the masculine/yang energy in so many ways at the expense of the feminine/yin that we are slowly killing ourselves, and slowly destroying our planet, our Mother Earth.

The systems and rules we have created for living our lives leave us feeling haggard, empty, eternally striving for something we can't quite seem to achieve. Is it deeper meaning we yearn for? Inner peace? Soulful fulfillment? Joyful connection?

Do we yearn for those missing elements enough that we are willing to make changes in the way we live our lives? One by one, little by little, we all must begin to dip our toes back into the waters of the feminine/yin. Infused back into the fabric of our lives, the masculine then becomes *sacred*, the feminine – *divine*.

Rebalancing our Relationship with Time

One of the ways we can begin to rebalance our relationship with the masculine/yang and feminine/yin forces at play, and thereby rebalance our lives and our world, is by examining our relationship with Father Time – Chronos time – and choosing to create the space for Kairos time in our lives.

Kairos time is slowness, it is depth. It doesn't have an agenda. It is immeasurable by any tangible means, but by joy in the soul and peace in the heart. It is experienced in those moments when we feel like everything is going to be ok. Those moments when we connect with something deep, something great, something that lives inside of ourselves, and also something much greater than ourselves.

Only from this place can we even begin to imagine treating ourselves, each other, and our Mother Earth in a way that isn't destructive. Only from this place can we begin the process of re-nourishing what we have been destroying and re-connecting what we have seen as separate, both internally within ourselves and externally in our lives and our society.

Kairos time is time that gives and nourishes, rather than takes and depletes. When we return to Chronos time, we are reminded that the clock keeps ticking on and we must make peace with that as well, but those immeasurable moments inside of Kairos time do more to nourish the soul than Chronos time ever will. If Chronos time binds us to the fact that eventually one day our human parts will die, it is Kairos time that allows us to touch the spirit and feel fully ALIVE while we are here.

-AUGUST PRACTICE-

ENJOY A KAIROS MOMENT: DIGITAL DETOX DAY

When summer begins to wane, and you're cursing how quickly time flies, this is the perfect opportunity to examine your very relationship with time itself. This month, enjoy a digital detox day, solo or with your loved ones! Let Kairos time infuse each precious moment with slowness and depth.

How can YOU start to slow down, carve out downtime and white space in your calendar, and begin to seek out and welcome in the Kairos moments in your own life?

This month, I encourage you to pick one day for a Digital Detox Day. What does this mean? This means that for one day you exist in the world without any technology, including clocks. No clocks, no Chronos time!

So, I recommend you do this on a day when you don't have to work so that you don't lose your job. If you have others living in your household with you – partners, children, parents – I recommend you get them in on it! This is an awesome way to have some unique quality time together. Even if you tend to drive each other crazy, this extreme change in routine creates a whole new way of experiencing each other and life, and it can be a lot of fun.

Digital Detox Day: The Ground Rules

RULE #1: The night prior, right before you go to bed, cover up all the clocks in your house with tape or sticky notes. When you wake up the next morning, you don't want to be able to see the clocks.

RULE #2: Here's the tricky one...the night prior, turn off your phones. And keep them off for the entire next day. Now, I understand not wanting to be completely un-reachable, so here are some ways to abate any fears you have around that.

If you're the emergency contact for someone – like an elderly parent or a kid off at college – and you don't want to be completely disconnected – give them ahead of time one number where they can reach you. Here's a straightforward way to do it: choose one cell phone in the house that you leave on and place somewhere where you could hear it ring. But put that phone somewhere out of reach, like inside a Tupperware container, or on the very top of a cabinet – so you can't just auto-reach for it throughout the day. Then set a specific ringtone for those contacts that might be contacting you in the case of an emergency only (Google *how to set a specific ringtone for a contact*). That way you don't need to look at your phone and spoil the time-less magic every time a spammer calls your phone. If you hear that specific ringtone, you can answer your phone. Otherwise, you get to be phone-free all day!

Ok, got it? I don't want this to feel overly complicated, but I also don't want it to be a day where you're nervous and worried about who can't reach you. I want you to feel free and spacious and able to set those cares aside! If there's no one that would be contacting you in the case of an emergency, just shut that phone off and you're good to go.

RULE #3: No peeking at the time during the day. Today, we're avoiding anything that has a clock on it, which is everything these days. Hide your watch the night before, make sure the clock on your coffee maker, oven, toaster, etc. are all covered. And no peeking at any technology that might give away the time. We're taking a total break from Chronos time today!

RULE #4: No using technology in the form of phones, laptops, tablets, TV, movies, social media, video games, and even...music. No Netflix, no Spotify, no Instagram, definitely no news. It might sound intense, but we're allowing ourselves a day to detox from our constant engagement with technology and the digital world.

How often do you find yourself mindlessly scrolling social media; watching something stressful on TV while you eat; bonding with your loved ones over a movie; filling the white space of your inner world with constant music? There is nothing wrong with these activities, necessarily! But the draw of technology is so strong that it tends to become a habit at best, a compulsion at worst.

Have you ever sat down to read a book, only to get immediately distracted by your phone? Had a free night with your partner for some quality time only to end up in front of the TV? Created a delicious and nourishing meal only to ruin it by watching the stressful news as you eat?

It's so easy for these things to occur! But not today, because we don't even have to make those choices today. The choice is made for us, which is easy and freeing.

I know some of you are still thinking...ok, but no music?! This is only a one-day break from habitually listening to music. You're completely free to get creative and *make* your own music on whatever real or made-up instruments you might enjoy!

RULE #5: Have fun. Be creative. Go outside. Laugh and play. Let some magic unfold. Here's the fun part: this is a day to live based on *how you feel*.

What time do you get up? Whenever you wake up. What time do you eat breakfast? Whenever you feel hungry. What time do you go to bed? Whenever you feel tired.

Interesting experiment, right? If you love to be spontaneous, this day is made for you. If you're more of a planner, take some time the day prior and make a list of all the activities you want to do but never have the time to do. But make sure it isn't just a list of chores around the house. Maybe it is a good time for some house projects, if that's what makes you happy and you just haven't found the time to get to them. For some people, that's their jam.

But make sure to also include things like going outside to walk or soak up some sun, cook a fun meal, do a crafty project, sing or make music on instruments or read a book. Maybe you want to meditate or do yoga, play a board game, or go pick flowers. Maybe you decide to go on a hike, run through the sprinkler, or watch the sunset. Or, do some conversation cards with your partner or kids for interesting deeper conversations than the usual, *"what time is dinner?"* conversations you tend to have on a regular, busy, time-driven day.

This is a day for whatever your heart and soul desires. For those moments of soul-nourishing Kairos time.

It's ok if all you want to do all day is absolutely nothing. Curl up in the sun for a cat nap, or relax on the couch and stare at the ceiling while you daydream. Doing nothing is one of the best ways to create the space for a spontaneous Kairos moment to find you.

This might also be a good day to ponder, have an interesting conversation about, or journal on those questions we posed earlier – I'll re-iterate them again here:

Questions to Ponder or Converse about:

- *Why is it hard for me to welcome in with open arms and joyful heart the season that allows us to move slower, do less, and self-reflect?*

- *Do I use busyness as a way to avoid looking at certain pieces of myself? Are there parts inside of myself that I'm hiding from? What pieces of myself am I afraid of confronting?*

- *What would have to change in my life in order to slow down? What would have to change in order to do less?*

- *How does the idea of slowing down and doing less make me feel? About myself? About my worth?*

- *Is my worth tied to my productivity? If I am not constantly being productive, do I believe I am not worthwhile?*

- *What moments of Kairos time am I keeping myself from experiencing?*

    o *Am I moving too fast to pause and truly take in a sunset? To truly stop and smell the flowers?*

    o *To breathe deeply enough to feel my breath all the way down in my belly?*

- o *To feel grateful for being here, being alive in this moment?*

- o *To sip my cup of tea or coffee and really taste it, really savor it?*

- o *To go so deep into a conversation that I completely lose track of time?*

Going Forward

At the end of the day, whenever you feel the sensation of tiredness and choose to go to bed, you are then free to remove the tape from all of your clocks and re-enter Chronos time!

Make sure you reflect on your experience of being untethered to Chronos time today. What did you learn? Would you do it again? If so, would you modify it in some way? Are there pieces of the experiment you feel inspired to incorporate into your daily life? More time for fun pursuits perhaps, or deep convos with loved ones, or time spent in nature? In what ways did your soul feel nourished today?

If you loved the experience, or felt intrigued enough to try it again, I encourage you to make it a ritual – weekly, monthly, seasonally – whatever feels right to you.

Happy Late Summer, friends! May you welcome in this season of slowing down, and begin carving out the white space in your calendar. In so doing, may you find and welcome in many Kairos moments to nourish your soul!

PART III

LATE SUMMER & AUTUMN

Late Summer & Autumn Intro: Balancing Light & Dark

WELCOME TO AUTUMN, FALL – the beginning of the yin cycle and *"new yin"* energy. My personal favorite season! The season of slowing down, turning inward, releasing heat after the bright fire and light of the summer. A time of golden hues, crunchy leaves, and yeah, pumpkin spice everything. What's not to love? But first...Late Summer. Last month we entered this little known fifth season as the month of August began to wane. But in case your journey is just beginning here, let's briefly explore, or review, what this mysterious little season is all about. In Chinese Five-Element Theory, there are five elements present in the makeup of everything around us, whose characteristics exist within us as well: Metal, Water, Wood, Fire and Earth. And those five elements correlate to five seasons: Fall, Winter, Spring,

Summer, and *Late Summer*. Late Summer is the short and sweet little season that starts around the last week of August and ends at the Fall Equinox in mid-September.

I've always thought the addition of this season makes so much sense. It helps to define the murky month of September – no longer summer, yet not quite fall. And it adds an important element to our experience of yin and yang energy – the element of *balance*. After the increasing yang of spring and summer, but before the deep yin of fall and winter, there is this moment of perfect balance, where yin and yang forces are nearly equal.

For us, on our journey, we'll use this time of perfect energetic balance to explore how to embody balance within our own lives. How do we achieve that elusive *"work-life balance"* that we all yearn for, but always seems just out of reach? During the month of September, you'll discover what it means to finally find – and sustain – true balance, from the inside out.

Then in October, as we're raking up the perfect pile of crunchy leaves for the kids to jump in, we'll explore what it means to play – as an adult. And how to truly infuse our lives with the energy of play. You'll also create your own play to-do list, which just might include jumping in that pile of leaves yourself. Sorry, kids!

And no exploration of the fall would be complete without a dive into the realm of darkness, as we explore the topics of death and letting go during the month of November. You'll gain a list of ten bizarre rituals to start engaging with – and making peace with – the elements of death and letting go in your own life.

May you enjoy this nourishing time of the year, and find a lasting sense of balance, playfulness, and peace in letting go.

CHAPTER 7

September: Discovering True Balance

SPRING AND SUMMER HAVE BEEN our time of growth and change and vitality – in nature, but within ourselves as well. They are times of new life, of turning outward, of going and doing and socializing, of big dreams and bold energy. While Autumn, on the other hand, is our time to embrace slowing down and turning inward. It's a harder sell in our overly-yang American culture, but it is our necessary time for reflection, introspection, and letting go of what no longer serves us. Just as we can't enjoy the day without the night to rest ourselves, we too can't fully enjoy the times of growth and outward expansion in our lives without equal time for rest, contemplation, and renewal.

And if we allow ourselves to live in alignment with the natural cycles of life – and not feel separate from them as though we are not a part of the whole web of nature – we may find that this time of year it can actually *feel good* to slow down, turn inward, and do less.

But before we shift into this time of darkness for rest, renewal and introspection, we have a moment to celebrate a time of complete balance. The short and sweet season of Late Summer serves as the perfect cushion between the fiery outward-facing energy of summer and the cool dark of autumn. And it allows for yin and yang energy to slowly start melding together without it having to feel like such a harsh transition.

This moment of balance culminates mid-month with the Fall Equinox, typically occurring around September 22 or 23. The Fall Equinox marks an especially balanced time of year — a time of equal day and night within a time of equal yin and yang energy. To further steep us in feelings of balance this month, we will also soon enter Libra season. On the same day as the Fall Equinox, the Sun will enter the sign of Libra in the astrological calendar. Represented by the symbol of the scales, Libra strives for balance between polarities. Its ultimate goal is equilibrium, harmony. And we can use this balanced energy around us to our advantage as we finally learn the trick to achieving that elusive sense of balance in our own lives.

Written in our Cells

The Tao Te Ching is an ancient book of wisdom written by the great spiritual teacher Lao Tzu. In one of my favorite modern translations of the work, *A Path and a Practice: Using Lao-tzu's Tao Te Ching as a Guide to an Awakened Spiritual Life,* author William Martin eloquently speaks to the concepts of yin and yang in verse 42:

> "Yin and yang together produce the energy of creation and give rise to all things. Every atom of the cosmos contains the yin and the yang together. We feel this harmonious process in the rising and falling of our breath."[30]

Isn't this a fascinating idea? *"Every atom of the cosmos contains the yin and the yang together."* That no matter how far our society may attempt to lean into yang energy alone – celebrating our outward achievements, but not our inner personal growth; praising making things happen, but not learning to let things come to us; encouraging going at Mach 2 speed with our hair on fire, but not slowing down and just *being* – still, within every cell of our bodies, there is both yin and yang.

And as we've been learning through our journey thus far, yin and yang energy balance each other, support each other, keep each other in check. When we're hot, we seek cold; when we're cold, we seek heat. When it's too bright out, we seek shade; when it's too dark out, we turn on a light. We are forever seeking to regain balance.

As articulated in the above verse, *"we feel this harmonious process in the rising and falling of our breath."* Martin's interpretation of Lao Tzu's words paints a beautiful picture to remind us that even through the simplest of acts – breathing – we seek balance. We breathe in, and we breathe out. We do this all day long, in equal measure. No matter how hard you may try, no one can survive on only breathing in or only breathing out! It's no wonder we're constantly after this elusive thing we call *balance*; it is written into our very cells.

Seeking Externally

"I just need to find some balance." I've heard this statement many times before! From clients, friends and family, even leaving my very own lips. I'm sure you've heard or said it, too. But if the concept of balance is written into our very cells, then *why* does it always feel so elusive, just out of reach, and impossible to maintain?

I think it's because we go about it the wrong way. Balance isn't meant to be something we seek at all; it's not something we're going to find outside of ourselves. Balance is meant to be something we *embody*. Seeking implies an external component; the greatest seekers eventually come to find that we have everything we need within us. Balance is no different. Striving for balance externally when we are not balanced internally – will be fruitless and unsustainable. Natural and sustainable balance comes from the inside out. As esteemed spiritual teacher Sadhguru has astutely pointed out, *"there is no such thing as work-life balance – it is all life. The balance has to be within you."*[31]

Internal Harmony

Another fancy word for balance is *"harmony."* And what is the definition of harmony? From the Cambridge and Oxford English Dictionaries, it is:

1. *"An agreement of ideas, feelings, or actions, or a pleasing combination of different parts."*[32]
2. *"The combination of separate but related parts in a way that uses their similarities to bring unity."*[33]
3. *"The quality of forming a pleasing and consistent whole."*[34]

When we harmonize our own many *"separate but related parts,"* we therefore bring equilibrium, wholeness, and balance into our lives. And we do this not by re-arranging the pieces of our external lives, but by re-arranging the pieces of our internal world.

What *"separate but related parts"* of our inner world can we bring into harmonious balance? We can start by looking at the more masculine/yang parts of our inner world and our personality, as well as the more feminine/yin parts. As a reminder, when we speak about masculine or feminine energy, it doesn't have anything to do with our gender. Masculine is another word for yang energy and feminine is another word for yin energy – and as we've learned, we are every single one of us made up of a collection of both kinds of energy. And we become *"a pleasing and consistent whole"* when we integrate both!

Honoring the Gift

There is a great saying that is often attributed to Einstein: *"The intuitive mind is a sacred gift and the rational mind is a faithful servant. We have created a society that honors the servant and has forgotten the gift."*[35] How balanced are YOU with your rational and intuitive sides? Do you, too, honor the servant and forget about the gift?

It's really through no fault of our own. We grow up going to school where there is only one way of knowing that is taught – through the rational mind. We learn to devalue the gift of our intuition; we stop seeing it as another useful way of knowing. We learn that any intuitive inclination must be backed up with a thousand rational thoughts for it to even begin to be seen as valid.

We are encouraged to develop the more masculine/yang traits of our personalities – our extraverted sides, our sensing abilities, our thinking minds, our ability to form conclusions and solidify our beliefs and opinions. It is seen as a positive in our culture to rely exclusively on five sensory perception, logic, and rationale; to be organized, a planner, in control; to be loud and take up space, to speak much and do constantly.

We are likewise discouraged from developing the more feminine/yin traits of our personalities – our introverted sides, our intuiting abilities, our feelings and emotional intelligence, our ability to be curious, to ask questions and keep a wildly open mind. It can be seen as a negative or a weakness to lean on intuitive knowing, to look beneath the surface of the apparent facts; to bring the heart and emotions into the picture; to be quiet, to listen and be receptive; to ask questions and *not* know; to be spontaneous and without a plan; to move slowly and do less.

But when we undervalue the gifts of the feminine/yin and overvalue our masculine/yang qualities, we live only from the physical body and the mind; and we disconnect ourselves from our heart and our soul and our spirit. But it is in valuing ALL of our many "separate but related parts" that we begin to eke our way once again towards this elusive idea of balance.

What Brings us Life

> *"We practice with the visible and tangible,*
> *but it is the invisible and intangible within us*
> *that bring us life."*

> *From Tao Te Ching Verse 11*
> *(William Martin translation)*[36]

In verse 11 of the Tao Te Ching, Lao Tzu and his many modern translators explore the opposing concepts of form vs. emptiness, matter vs. space, outer vs. inner, without vs.

within, visible vs. invisible, tangible vs. intangible. The idea is proposed that while we tend to interact with and be most aware of the outer, tangible and visible aspects of things, it is actually the inner, formless and invisible aspects that are perhaps the most essential.

We are encouraged here to look beyond the surface of what we see in order to assess the true value of anything. As Lao Tzu goes on to explain in this verse, we must remember that the wheel appears useful because of its visible spokes, yet it is the invisible space in the center that allows it to spin. That a bowl appears useful because of its concrete form, but the bowl is only useful to us because of the empty space within. That a house appears useful because of its outer walls and roof, but it is the vacant space within that allows life to flourish there.

This teaching encourages us to remember that it is not only the true value of any*thing* that we can see by looking more deeply into the inside, but also the true value of any*one*. What are the visible, outer aspects of ourselves that we are perhaps the most attuned to and aware of? These are typically the more yang/masculine parts that keep us moving forward, going, doing, building, organizing, making. And what are the invisible, inner aspects of ourselves that we can only see by looking more deeply? These are typically the more yin/feminine parts that allow us tap into our inner desires, feelings, inspirations, and intuitions. As Martin's translation of this verse puts it so beautifully, *"we practice with the visible and tangible, but it is the invisible and intangible within us that bring us life."* What a shame it would be to live our lives as an incredibly useful but empty container, and to neglect the very parts of ourselves that fill us with life!

As we welcome in this dark part of the year and honor the gifts that darkness brings to our external lives –

permission to slow down and do less, for example – we can also use this time to welcome in our own inner dark parts. Those parts represented by having a more yin quality, as well as those that might be hiding just out of our awareness in our shadow – and honor the gifts they, too, hold.

If both yin and yang energy are written into our very cells, we don't have to think of it as creating something entirely new or foreign to our way of being when we start to bring in the yin elements of our personality and inner world. Instead, we are simply allowing the space for this energy *already within us* to be expressed. We are giving ourselves permission at last to experience, or *embody*, true balance. To unknowingly stop fighting so hard against the idea of balance, and at last allow ourselves to be *filled with life.*

Balancing Our Yin & Yang Parts

Yin and yang are relative terms, not absolutes – meaning everything is yin or yang relative *to* something else. The moon is yin relative to the yang of the sun; but the full moon is actually quite yang relative to the yin of the dark new moon. The bright hot sun seems like it would clearly be all yang, but a sunset is quite yin relative to the full yang peak of the midday sun.

And the bright full moon within the dark of night is a good example of *"yang within yin"* – another idea represented in the yin-yang symbol via the white dot within the black half of the circle. The setting sun during the last hours of daytime is a good example of *"yin within yang"* – the idea represented by the small black dot within the white half of the yin-yang symbol. All this to say – there is no one, and no thing, that is entirely ALL yin or ALL yang. We are all, as the definition of harmony suggests: *"a pleasing combination of different parts."*

But to keep things simple, I think it can be helpful to take some of our many separate but related parts and classify them as more yin or more yang – so we can see where our own scales might be out of balance and where we might need to draw in some of the opposite qualities in order to regain a sense of equilibrium.

And just like last month's exploration of the more masculine/yang concept of Chronos time and the more feminine/yin concept of Kairos time, where we noted that of course we need *both* in our lives in order to fully function as individuals and as a society – we of course here, too, need *both* of our more masculine/yang traits and our more feminine/yin traits in order to fully function. The point isn't to overvalue the feminine/yin and undervalue the masculine/yang – we don't need to create another kind of imbalanced life or society! It's just that our current lives and society tend to skew so harshly in the direction of overvaluing only the gifts of the masculine/yang, that the current medicine lies in integrating more of the feminine/yin.

So, what yin characteristics are you keeping in your shadow that are perhaps being over-shadowed by the bright spotlight on your yang traits? Consider the following suggestions and ponder where you can bring more of your own yin qualities out of the dark to create more harmony and balance in your life:

- If you've mastered rational thinking, can you bring your ability to know something intuitively out of the shadows?

- If you rely on being logical, can you bring your feeling side out of the shadows?
- If you excel at turning outward and honoring your extraverted parts, can you turn inward and bring your quiet introverted side out of the shadows?
- If you naturally enjoy making decisions and closing loops, can you bring your desire to be wildly curious and expand what you think you know out of the shadows?
- If you're good at moving quickly in actions and decisions, can you bring your ability to pause and slow things down out of the shadows?
- If you're always getting things done and being productive, can you bring the side of you that loves to play and do nothing out of the shadows?

Changing Our World, Changing the World

We must find ways to make space for and honor the feminine/yin parts of ourselves – for if we don't honor our natural cellular makeup of both yin and yang, we will forever feel that balance is something that eludes us, remains just out of reach. But once we allow for our personal scales to rebalance, we will finally feel like a harmonious *"pleasing and consistent whole."*

Though it is society itself that pushes our internal scales out of balance – by solely pushing the agenda of the yang/masculine/rational – the only way to change society is by first changing ourselves. And when you begin to wonder, am I really making any difference in the world by just changing myself? The answer is yes! Because what if you, and that person, and that person, and another few hundred or thousands of people are thinking the same exact thing? I don't tend to believe that top-down changes are sustainable – or they just give an illusion of change, with a bunch of unhappy people feeling constrained by rules pushed upon them. It is change made from the bottom up *that truly shifts a society*. And bottom-up change starts with the individual. As cliché as it sounds, it does start with you.

It might take embodying a little bit of the Maverick archetype energy – a little piss and vinegar – to stand strong in the face of a society that doesn't support your changes at first. To say – ok, enough! I'm going to live my life differently! More...slowly. And beautifully. And intuitively. But know that when you give yourself permission to change, you give everyone around you permission as well. Come on, think of the ripple effect. And you thought you were just one person.

The most important thing to remember in all of this is that no matter how much we try and re-arrange the pieces of our external lives to create the conditions that we think should bring us the feeling of balance...it will forever be impossible to maintain, it will forever feel just out of reach – if it doesn't arise first from *within* us.

-SEPTEMBER PRACTICE-

LIMITING BELIEFS QUIZ + SHADOW WORK

This season of outward energetic balance is an ideal time to explore how to embody balance within your own life. Spend some time contemplating the questions that follow, and deeply examining the beliefs and behaviors that may be keeping you stuck in a cycle of imbalance.

Part 1 - Limiting Beliefs Quiz:

This quiz helps us to answer the question, *in what ways do I unknowingly prevent myself from embodying balance in my own life?* Be honest with yourself – this quiz is for you and you alone (or maybe your therapist, coach or healer if you want to share with them for extra support). No one is here to judge you, and there are no extra points for making yourself look better. You'll benefit the most from this quiz when you can be incredibly honest about where you're at right now.

Reflect on the following questions and answer each with *yes, no,* or *sometimes.* I suggest writing your answers down, as you'll need that information for Part 2.

1. Do I believe I am only worthwhile when I am productive and get a lot done?
2. Do I feel disappointed, frustrated, or worthless when I don't get everything done on my to-do list?

3. Do I often ignore my feelings and desires in favor of being "practical?"
4. Do I disregard my intuition if it doesn't seem "logical?"
5. Do I feel uncomfortable or bored when I slow down, and consciously or subconsciously make myself get back into doing/going mode?
6. Do I feel beholden to my to-do lists and struggle with allowing myself to do less?
7. Do I override my introverted preferences and needs because my extraverted qualities seem more acceptable and "get me ahead?"
8. Do I have a hard time letting go of control?
9. Am I a perfectionist?
10. Do I have a hard time enjoying relaxing until all my tasks are completed first?
11. When I have downtime or free-time to relax or play, do I often end up working on house tasks, work tasks, or my to-do list?
12. Do I have a hard time making time for my hobbies?
13. Do I feel self-conscious when I don't know something, or have a hard time saying "I don't know?"
14. Do I feel embarrassed sharing my feelings with others?
15. Do I have a hard time acknowledging that I actually have feelings, or that those feelings can be hurt?

Part 2 - Create a List

What are the limiting beliefs and behaviors that keep me stuck in a cycle of imbalance?

Look back over the quiz and revisit the questions that you answered with a "yes" or "sometimes." These questions give you clues as to the limiting beliefs and behaviors that are keeping you stuck in a cycle of imbalance.

In your journal, make a list of these limiting beliefs and behaviors that you resonated with from the quiz. For example, if you answered "yes" or "sometimes" to the first five questions in the quiz, you might write something in your journal like:

- *My worth is tied up in my productivity.*
- *I feel frustrated and worthless when I don't get everything done on my to-do list.*
- *I often ignore my feelings in order to be practical.*
- *I will disregard my intuition when it doesn't seem logical.*
- *I get bored and uncomfortable when I slow down, and will pretty quickly get back into going/doing mode.*

Write down all of them that apply to you, whether it's one belief/behavior or all 15 – however you want to word the beliefs/behaviors in a way that personalizes them to you.

Part 3 - Shadow Work: Getting to the Root of the Beliefs/Behaviors

What is Shadow Work?

Shadow work simply means that we are consciously willing to look at the parts of ourselves that we keep hidden in the dark, or in our shadow. The term *"shadow"* in a psychological context comes from Carl Jung's work and refers to the parts of our psyche that we reject from our consciousness.[37] There are parts of ourselves that we deem acceptable, and we keep those out in the open, in the light, for regular public and personal consumption – in Jungian terms this is called our "persona." And then there are parts of ourselves that we may unconsciously deem unacceptable, and so we tuck those down real deep into the corners and crevices of our soul and psyche and try to keep those parts from being seen by others. This creates our shadow.

We also try to keep those parts from being seen by *ourselves*, but it's a funny thing trying to stay blind to something within your own self. Whether or not we like those parts of ourselves, they are a part of the whole puzzle that makes us who we are – and when we cut ourselves off from any part of ourselves, we prevent ourselves from ever feeling truly whole and complete. But the other funny thing is that once we finally look at those parts that we've spent so much energy relegating to the shadows, and we make peace with them, and re-integrate them into the whole of who we are – we usually feel a whole lot better. And we free up a lot of energy that was previously being used for keeping those parts at bay.

It's not easy to look at parts of ourselves that we have deemed unacceptable or ugly or shameful – but being on this journey of self-discovery, soul-care, and spiritual awakening, I know that you are a courageous being who wants nothing more than to feel better, complete and whole. You can do this alone, but you can also do it with a trusted guide like a therapist or coach if you feel better having that extra support.

Shadow work is deep self-reflection. And what better time to engage in this work than during the season that marks the beginning of the dark cycle, the season that encourages us to turn within and take a deep look at our inner selves?

The How-To

Return to your list of limiting beliefs/behaviors that you made in Step 2. The next step is to become curious as to the root cause of this list of limiting beliefs/behaviors that you now have written down in your journal. We'll get curious by asking the following questions:

1. *Where did these beliefs/behaviors come from?*
2. *When did they originate?*
3. *Why did they continue to operate?*
4. *What purpose do they serve in my life?*
5. *How do they keep me safe?*

So, for each one of the limiting beliefs/behaviors that you have written down, take a moment to ask yourself those questions and allow yourself to reflect. You might find that one of these beliefs or behaviors popped up recently, due to something that someone – like a boss or colleague or partner – said to you, that caused you to start acting in a certain way. But more likely, you'll have to allow your mind and heart to travel farther back in time, maybe to your childhood, where many of our limiting beliefs first took root.

For example, let's take the first one on our list: *'my worth is tied up in my productivity.'*

Ask yourself each self-reflection question and write down anything that comes to mind. We'll go through each question together below using this example belief so you can get a feel for the whole process.

1. **WHERE DID THIS BELIEF COME FROM?** Maybe you saw your parents model this same belief and behavior, or maybe you received a lot of praise when you worked hard and brought back good grades or other accolades, or received disapproval when you didn't.

2. **WHEN DID THIS BELIEF ORIGINATE?** Maybe you can remember a specific moment in time, in third grade when you brought back a bad grade and got a scolding from a parent, or forgot to turn in your homework and were shamed by a teacher; maybe it's more of a general feeling of a time period when you remember starting to act in this way.

3. **WHY DID THIS BELIEF CONTINUE TO OPERATE?** Maybe this belief continued to operate because you continued to receive reinforcement for it, getting praise for working hard and getting a lot done, and receiving disapproval for doing less, "slacking," or playing or daydreaming when a teacher or parent thought you should have been working.

4. **WHAT PURPOSE DOES THIS BELIEF SERVE IN MY LIFE?** Maybe it keeps you in a good, high paying job where you don't have to worry about slacking off and losing your

job. Maybe it keeps your house spotless and organized at all times so that the clutter never makes you feel chaotic.

5. **HOW DOES THIS BELIEF KEEP ME SAFE?** Maybe it keeps you financially safe because your job that requires a lot of work also gives you a lot of money and nice health insurance. Maybe it keeps you socially safe because you gain respect and approval for the position you hold. Maybe it keeps you emotionally safe because it prevents you from ever having to feel worthless, which is how you feel if you stop working so hard.

Go through this practice with each of your limiting beliefs and behaviors now. If you answered "yes" or "sometimes" to a lot of the beliefs/behaviors from the quiz (this is normal) and you're feeling overwhelmed about going through this process for *all* of them, pick out 3 that feel like a big part of your life, and start there. You can always come back to the others at a later time if you feel called to do so.

Think of each one of these beliefs/behaviors as an operating program that has been controlling your thoughts and actions from the background for a very long time. But remember that you never gave permission for any of this software to run! It's time to start asking some questions about the nature and motives of these programs that are running you, and deciding if it's time for a system upgrade.

Part 4: Self-Permission

How can I give myself permission to embody balance?

Remember, as we said earlier, we all hold the key to balance written into our very being – we are a collection of both yin and yang energy. So, we don't have to try and create out of nothing some brand new way of being; instead, we are simply allowing the space for this energy already within us to be expressed.

We are giving ourselves permission at last to experience, or embody, true balance. To unknowingly stop fighting so hard against the idea of balance, and at last allow ourselves to be *filled with life.*

Imagine that this idea of balance applies to every one of your limiting beliefs and behaviors. What if a particular belief or behavior is expressing as one possible way of operating in the world, but its exact opposite also already lives within you?

Then changing these beliefs and behaviors would be less of an exercise in overcoming, controlling and striving towards balance, and more of a practice in expressing something that lives inside of us, that previously hasn't been allowed to be expressed.

And the key wouldn't be in employing more and more masculine/yang energy to force the new behavior to happen, but in embodying feminine/yin energy to allow this new behavior to unfold. The key would be giving ourselves permission for this previously unacceptable side of ourselves to once again see the light of day.

So, now that you've started to poke holes into these previously subconscious operating systems that have been controlling your behavior from the background, go back to this list of limiting beliefs and write its opposite.

For example, let's take the first five again:

- **OLD BELIEF:** *My worth is tied up in my productivity.*
  - ○ **NEW BELIEF:** *My worth is inherent. I am worthy just by nature of being here on this earth!*

- **OLD BELIEF:** *I feel frustrated and worthless when I don't get everything done on my to-do list.*
  - ○ **NEW BELIEF:** *Even when I don't finish everything on my to-do list, I still feel worthwhile and take time to feel gratitude for everything I did complete that day.*

- **OLD BEHAVIOR:** *I often ignore my feelings in order to be practical.*
  - ○ **NEW BEHAVIOR:** *I listen to my feelings and treat them as the sacred messengers of my soul that they are, and I also listen to my rational brain thoughts. I allow both sources of information to be held in high esteem. When I need a tie-breaker, I listen to my intuition.*

- **OLD BEHAVIOR:** *I will disregard my intuition when it doesn't seem logical.*
  - ○ **NEW BEHAVIOR:** *I know that my intuition won't always seem "logical" yet I*

> *will still trust that it is somehow guiding me*
> *towards what is best for my highest self.*

- **OLD BEHAVIOR:** *I get bored and uncomfortable when I slow down, and will pretty quickly get back into going/doing mode.*
  - **NEW BEHAVIOR:** *I notice the boredom and discomfort that occurs when I slow down, and I get curious about it, ask it where it's coming from and why, and I know that it's ok to feel bored and uncomfortable because it's probably trying to teach me something about myself.*

Now, do this for yourself. Go through and re-write each limiting belief and behavior on your list (or re-write the top 3 that you've chosen to work with currently). You have the power to create the operating system that you DO want running you! So, create an operating system that makes your soul happy.

Going Forward

You may find that this is a practice you want to take slowly, and choose to only look at one limiting belief/behavior at a time. Shadow work isn't something we do just one time, it's a journey of re-integrating bits and pieces of ourselves in service to our wholeness. So, much like our whole journey this year, let it be a slow and sustainable journey!

I also recommend going back and revisiting this often during this month, even throughout this year, to keep reminding yourself of these new beliefs and behaviors you've written out. Just because we write down our NEW beliefs and behaviors doesn't mean they will immediately feel true or become automatic habits. We have a lifetime of old ways of being, and it will take some time to make those shifts to our internal beliefs and external actions. So, be kind to yourself! And, it's helpful to keep them top of mind and take steps to notice when you're falling back into the old patterns.

Also, this book contains a few practices that really focus on different aspects of letting go and scouring our energetic slate clean, such as the practices in Chapters 2 and 9 during the months of April and November. Practices like that will work together with practices like this to remove the old programming, helping to clear space for the new to take root.

Happy Late Summer and early Autumn, friends! As you go forth, may you enjoy this time of perfect external balance – and let it inspire you to rebalance your own internal scales, creating a lasting harmony from the inside out.

CHAPTER 8

October: Remembering (How) to Play

WITH THE LEAVES FALLING from the trees, this time of year always makes me think about the quintessential childhood activity of raking up a giant pile of leaves just to jump in it. To the adults, it's a great way to get those pesky leaves gathered up so they can be more efficiently bagged. But to the kids, the sole purpose is: *play*. But how many of us grow up and still see the playful possibilities in a pile of leaves?

There was a recent beautiful fall day when I was outside watering my new landscaping. While accomplishing my useful adult task, I was also watching four little kids across the street playing in their yard. I couldn't tell you what they were doing – some version of yoga/martial arts/dragging each other across the grass? But that's the point – as children we don't need to define what playing is, we just go outside, let our imaginations take over, and get weird with it. But, somewhere along the way, it seems we stop knowing how to get weird with it.

A Lifetime of Choosing Between Work and Play

I was eight years old when I first consciously discovered stress, expectations, being responsible – and having to choose between work and play. I remember it clearly. My 3rd grade teacher always gave us copious amounts of homework, and being as thorough and meticulous as I was, I could never seem to get it all done. I'd be inside working away for hours, listening to the rest of the neighborhood kids playing outside and squealing with delight.

Thankfully my mom saw this problem and came to my rescue. She started sending me to school with notes for my teacher: *"Dear Mrs. So and So, Angela did not finish her homework because she worked on it for this many hours and then I sent her outside to play."* Was it just me? Even decades later with much consciousness around not letting my perfectionist tendencies get out of hand, I am still thorough, meticulous, and think about things deeply – which are great qualities, but also translate into taking a long time to finish things. Or...was it just my early initiation into a culture where we will spend the rest of our lives choosing between work and play?

We all know the common proverb: *All work and no play makes Jack a dull boy.*[38] So then why does our culture put such a high value on work, forcing us so often to choose between work and play?

Childhood: Keepin' it Weird

In my work with my coaching clients, we'll often come up with assignments based around these six pillars: Gratitude, Quiet, Nature, Intuition, Self-Care, and Play. And *play*...seems to be the hardest assignment for people! It seems that as adults, we've almost completely forgotten what it really means to play.

I recently came across one of many notebooks from my childhood that contained some of my "to-do" lists. For research purposes, I'd like to take you on a little journey into the mind of a – *very detail-oriented* – child as we try to remember once again the meaning of "play."

Exhibit A from my childhood notebook:

"LIST OF WHAT WE CAN DO"

1. *Play outside or inside*
2. *Play Pony's*
3. *Play Barbies*
4. *Dress up and put makeup on and go to a place*
5. *Have babies and play house*
6. *Play game inside or outside*
7. *Play on swing set*
8. *Play on beach*
9. *Roll down the hill*
10. *Have a nature walk*
11. *Play fashion girls*
12. *Play store*
13. *Have a play*

What I love about this particular "to-do" list is that it's really just 13 different ways to play!

Exhibit B from my childhood notebook:

"THINGS TO DO AT THE SLEEPOVER"

1. *Unpack and get bed ready*
2. *Play for a little bit*
3. *Eat dinner*
4. *Movie or T.V. (Play)*
5. *Get ready for bed*
6. *Get in bed and read*
7. *Lights out*
8. *Talk for a little bit*
9. *Try to get to sleep*

You may have noticed that this sleepover itinerary (the detailed itinerary is standard sleepover practice, right?) contains not one, but TWO instances of play.

And, lastly, Exhibit C from my childhood notebook:

"MORNING"

1. *Watch TV*
2. *Eat breakfast*
3. *Get dressed*
4. *The rest of the day, plan what we are going to do while the day is going.*

That last one seems to be my hyper-organized child-brain interpretation of the idea: just be spontaneous. Which also feels like a roundabout way of trying to say: *play!*

Thanks to my childhood propensity for list-making, we can see that the importance of play is so CLEAR to us as children. Even to very organized, detail-oriented children, play makes the list again and again. So, the question is, can we remember once again as adults what it means to play?

What is Play?

So, let's go back to the beginning. What exactly IS play? The Oxford Languages dictionary defines play as: *"activity for enjoyment and recreation rather than a serious or practical purpose,"* and adds that it is engaged in, *"especially by children."*[39] But we're about to change that *"especially by children"* part because my goal by the end of this chapter is to get you and your adult brain excited again about the idea of play.

Some other ways we might define play are: *amusement, entertainment, recreation, enjoyment, pleasure, diversion, leisure, fun, games, horseplay, revelry, living it up* – and my personal favorites: *jollification and merrymaking.* We can *go play,* or we can: *have fun, have a good time, amuse oneself, enjoy oneself, be at leisure, frolic, or romp.* Have you frolicked or romped lately?

And the definition of play lists the opposite of play as – you guessed it, work. But it's interesting to note that play researchers like Dr. Stuart Brown and the late Professor Brian Sutton-Smith have been pointing out that, actually, the opposite of play isn't work as we've all assumed, it's *depression.*[40] All work and no play makes Jack a dull boy...*because Jack is now depressed.* Far from frivolous or just for children, we can see that play is an essential and foundational aspect of our very wellbeing!

Dr. Brown, a psychiatrist, pioneering play researcher, and founder of the National Institute for Play, also defines play as something done for its own sake, meaning it doesn't have a particular purpose. He says that if the purpose is more important than the act of doing it, it's probably not play.[41] I think this is where we get into trouble as adults. It's hard to convince ourselves to engage in something that has no purpose! Recently the hubs was telling me about some of his coworkers who are in a fantasy football league. They all put in a hundred dollars and someone wins the pot at the end. I asked him what he thought their purpose was – was it to win the money or just for fun? I wondered if they would all still do it if there wasn't any prospect of winning money and it was just for the pure enjoyment of it.

What about the things that *you* engage in – do you go running because running is fun, or because it's good for your health? Do you do crossword puzzles because you love crossword puzzles, or because it promotes healthy brain function? Do you engage in fantasy football solely because it's fun, or because you could win some money?

When we're truly playing, it's about our love for the very thing we're engaging in – regardless of what the outcome may be. Of course, it's still ok to partake in those other outcome-driven activities, but it might be worth re-evaluating *why* we are doing the things we do, and discovering if there are other things we might be more excited to spend our time doing. Things that might even result in the same outcome, but with a much more enjoyable path to get there. For instance, if you want to promote a healthy lifestyle – a worthy outcome – but you hate running, what if you found a different activity that you *do* love doing? Something that feels like play *and* just happens to also support your health? Imagine the joy if we organized our whole life this way!

It's interesting to note that studies on play have also shown that play releases feel-good endorphins, improves memory, and stimulates the growth of the cerebral cortex. It helps us with stress management and even improves our relationships – laughing and having fun not only helps lighten our own burdens, but fosters empathy, compassion, trust and intimacy with others. And although we've said that true play has no purpose, I think that's a convincing enough list of desirable outcomes for our logical adult brains to get on board!

Creativity and Play

Ok, so we're once again interested in the concept of playing...but *how do we do that again?* Sure, we could roll down the hill or swing on a swing set, but most adults don't want to *"have babies and play house"* because that's just regular life. So, we can use my childhood lists for some inspiration, but we might need to get a little more creative about what play looks like for us now!

Speaking of needing to get creative, let's examine the very relationship between creativity and play. Dr. Brown says that from a neuroscience perspective, *"nothing lights up the brain like play."*[42] Specifically – our right brain lights up when we are playing. Whereas the left brain is our more masculine/yang, logical, analytical side, it is the right brain that is our more feminine/yin, intuitive, creative side. It makes sense that play, having no logical purpose or outcome, would be linked to our creative right brain.

Does it follow then, that if we've forgotten how to play, that we've also forgotten how to be creative? And if we allow ourselves once again to be creative, will we naturally remember how to play? It seems that creativity and play support each other, need each other. And creativity goes way beyond arts 'n crafts. It is the driving force that allows us to create what has never been created before, to imagine what has never been done before. As Carl Jung has said: *"the creation of something new is not accomplished by the intellect, but by the play instinct."*[43] Being creative – and therefore, being playful – improves our ability to solve novel problems; it means we're better able to be adaptable to whatever life throws at us. And in this ever-changing crazy world, that's something we could all use more of in our lives.

So How Do You Play?

With our right-brain creative juices flowing, and our left-brain motivation on board – let's get to the *how*. According to Dr. Brown, play isn't just one thing – there are actually multiple categories that we might engage in, such as:

- BODY PLAY – *physically engaging the body, or adrenaline-charged activities*
- OBJECT PLAY – *building or manipulating objects*
- SOCIAL PLAY – *playing with others*
- ROUGH AND TUMBLE PLAY – *physical play with others i.e. sports, wrestling around*
- SPECTATOR PLAY – *watching sports, watching others play*
- RITUAL PLAY – *contains rules and structure i.e. board games*
- IMAGINATIVE PLAY – *arts 'n crafts, comedy, improv, storytelling*

And with my own interest in understanding our unique personality/psychological type as a way to better understand ourselves (see Chapter 5 during the month of July for a deep-dive into this), I was delighted to learn that Dr. Brown has even identified eight different play personalities. To learn more about his playfully groundbreaking work, and to determine your own play personality, I would recommend visiting his website at nifplay.org.

Knowing your unique play personality could help you come up with ideas for what play can look like in your adult life, but the most important thing is just paying attention to those activities that naturally excite and energize you. One of the first questions I always ask someone when profiling for their psychological type – which is different from a play personality, although I definitely see some crossover! – is this: *what do you love to do?*

What are you doing when time just seems to fly by, when you look at your watch suddenly and realize three hours has passed and you forgot to eat or pee? What is it you love to do so much that you would keep doing it endlessly and joyfully until you finally reach exhaustion? Pay attention to all the details: when time flies by joyfully are you typically alone, or with others? Where are you, indoors or outdoors? And what is it that you're engaging in?

Answer these questions for yourself and you might find some big clues as to how you prefer to play! There are no right or wrong answers, and it definitely varies from person to person what play looks like in someone's adult life. What one person considers play, another person might find entirely boring or extremely stressful – just making it all the more important to dial into your unique mode of play.

Play vs. Rest

It's interesting to note that the dictionary also included rest and relaxation in their lists of synonyms for play. But I excluded these terms on purpose because I think it's important to differentiate play from rest and relaxation.

Because although our child brains didn't need any help defining the differences between work, play, and rest – I think our adult brains need to know!

As grownups with already too much to do, we might be tempted to smoosh play and rest into one singular category in order to best manage our seemingly limited resource of time. But while play and rest might be dear cousins, they each definitely deserve a dedicated place on our plates. We've already thoroughly defined play, so let's take a gander into the meanings of rest and relaxation, according to the Oxford Languages Dictionary:

> **Rest** *(verb): "to cease work or movement in order to relax, refresh oneself, or recover strength."*[44]

> **Relaxation** *(noun): "the state of being free from tension and anxiety."*[45]

And the synonyms of rest and relaxation include: *let up, slow down, pause, laze, idle, do nothing, unwind, recharge one's batteries, take it easy* – as well as *calm, tranquility, peacefulness, and unwinding.* I would personally categorize all of these concepts – rest, relaxation and yes, even play – as various manifestations of yin/being/non-doing energy. This is where they do share similarities. Compared to "work" and most tasks on our to-do lists – which have a very yang, achievement-oriented energy – rest *and* play are very yin in comparison.

But the difference I see is that rest/relaxation is yin/being/non-doing energy turned *inward* – nourishing to the body, heart, soul and spirit. A more or less complete ceasing of activity. We rest after we've worked hard. But we also rest after we've played hard – so they can't be the same thing. So, I think we can differentiate play as yin/being/non-doing energy directed *outward* – an expression of the body, heart, soul and spirit. It's active, yes, but activity stemming from *joy*.

Play: Balancing Force or Driving Force?

In our busy adult lives full of plenty of tasks that we must complete, we can often already feel stretched about finding the time for rest and relaxation, and we definitely don't want play to just feel like another thing we now have to take the time to *do*. I've definitely heard that from clients – and have been there myself, too. Our best healthy intentions and habits just end up as another task on the to-do list, driven more by the fear of not completing the task than by any feelings of passion or joy. But what if we didn't have to find a way to fit play into our already busy schedules? What if we could instead allow it to naturally seep into our everyday lives? To do this, we might need to rethink the way we view play altogether.

When I was in college, I found the level of work and stress really ramped up from the days of my third-grade woes. So, the level of play did, too. We all know the saying: *work hard, play hard.* But what is real play? Is it letting off steam? A release valve for the pressure of our busy lives? Simply a way to balance out all the work and stress we endure? Modern living has created lives that clearly need some amount of carved out time for play in order to feel balanced – but if we need this release valve and balancing force so badly in our lives, what is going on with the rest of our lives? Why are we allowing the other half of our lives to reach such an intense level of stress? Are we so unfulfilled or unhappy with this other half of our lives that we need to make up for it in equal doses of fun and excitement? Is it even sustainable to keep ramping up the levels of work and play? For me, eventually it wasn't and I burned out and got very sick.

I don't think that true play is meant to be just a release valve – I think it's something deeper, something much more vital to our wellbeing. What if play wasn't meant to be simply a balancing force for the out-of-whack other half of our lives, but instead the primary driving force that propels us forward through our whole lives? How would our lives look – and more importantly feel – differently if we were driven by the force of play rather than the force of striving, pushing, or proving? What if we still achieved big things, accomplished great feats, and showed the world our magic – but simply as the happy result of being driven by play?

Life Becomes Play

We've found that play has a close relationship to creativity. What about its relationship to joy? We learned that the opposite of play is depression – and we typically think of the opposite of depression as joy; therefore, it seems to suggest a deep similarity between the concepts of play and joy. Striving, forcing and proving are descendants of fear – and it doesn't feel good to live our lives driven from this place. Wouldn't it feel better to be driven by joy?

Last month, we explored the idea of perceiving every aspect of our lives as part of *life* itself, and to avoid seeing work and life as two opposing forces to be balanced. Similarly, instead of seeing work and play as two opposing forces to be balanced, we can choose instead to see everything in our lives as play. In this way, work becomes *life*, and life becomes *play*.

It's a revolutionary idea, isn't it? An idea with the potential to completely transform your life and your access to joy. In this way, play becomes much more than something to do in your spare time. It becomes something with the potential to completely rearrange your life and infuse it with passion and joy.

Putting it into Action

As adults we tend to make lists of what we must DO. Recently the hubs and I started a joint to-do list for all our various house and yard projects and tasks. The idea is that at the beginning of each month we assess the list, remove anything that has been completed or no longer feels relevant, and pick out a few projects for the upcoming month that get assigned to one or both of us. Then, we can put the list away until the next month to keep it from feeling like the endless pile of tasks that home ownership can sometimes feel like.

But, more recently I realized that we needed a second kind of list to assess each month, as well. The list of fun things to do. I was getting all these ideas for fun things to do, but then stressing myself out because we weren't doing them! So, we decided a monthly assessment of *fun things to do* would be useful as well. Why shouldn't we take our play lists just as seriously as we do our to-do lists? After all, we've discovered that play is essential to our happiness and wellbeing. My child-self showed us that a to-do list can certainly include not only one, but 13 ways to play. So, I challenge you to make your own list of fun ways to play, AND to take it as seriously as your to-do list!

But if you really want to revolutionize your life, start thinking about not only how you can add back in more ways to play, but how the very building blocks of your life can be *fueled* by what feels playful. What if family activities felt like playtime not only for the kids, but for the adults as well? What if date night felt like play? What if exercise felt like play? What if your very job felt like play?

Recently I've started playing around with activities that feel fun and joyful, like rollerskating and dance! It feels playful for my inner child and freeing for my adult self. It also *just happens* to be a surprisingly good workout – although I have to be careful to remember *that's not the point*, just a happy accident – otherwise it's easy for play activities to start to feel like just another task on the regular to-do list. If that happens to you, try to tune back into the motives of your inner child: did you used to run all over the yard and jump up and down in a pile of leaves because it was a good workout and would sculpt your ass? Or because it was just really fun?

That's one way I've started adding back ways to play. But I also make sure to *infuse* my life with the very driving force of play. Because I own my own business and have no one to blame but myself, anytime work starts to feel heavy, blah or uninspiring, I take it seriously and contemplate how I can mix things up again! I make myself come back to the idea of *what feels joyful and playful* a lot, so that I don't get too hard on myself about what I'm not achieving *yet* or think I should be achieving *now*. So that the process itself is still fun, regardless of the outcome.

As you journey forward into your own playful life, may you be inspired by the words of playwright George Bernard Shaw: *"We don't stop playing because we grow old; we grow old because we stop playing."*[46] So, now it's your turn – go forth and frolic, play and be merry!

-OCTOBER PRACTICE-

INFUSE YOUR LIFE WITH PLAY

October used to mean creating that perfect pile of crunchy leaves to jump in. Now, as an adult, it's the perfect time to re-examine what it means to play in your life. Create your own ultimate play to-do list, and discover what it means to infuse your life with the driving force of play.

To start, open your journal or get out a piece of paper and create two columns or sections. Label one: *What I love to do now*, and the other: *What I loved to do as a child*. Then, reflect on the following four prompts:

Question #1 - What do I love to do now?

As you may recall, this question was also addressed in the practice from Chapter 5 in the month of July. So, if you've been through that chapter already, you can revisit your answers to this question and add them to this month's list. If you're working – er, playing – your way through this journey in a different order, you can ponder the question now!

Even if you've already answered this question, feel free to ponder it again. With the change of seasons, maybe your answer has changed, too. Or expanded, as you've been on this journey for a few seasons now and have perhaps found even more things you love to do. If so, add them to your list!

This is such an important question for us to revisit. It seems so obvious that we should spend a lot of our time doing the things that we love – and yet, so often we don't.

We often relegate those things that we love to do the category of "nice to have." We put what we love to do in the play bucket, and decide we'll get to that *after* we've completed all our important work.

But our to-do lists can begin to take on a life of their own and become never-ending and all-consuming. If the work never ends, when we will get to the fun stuff?

And how often do we hear of people saving their big dreams for after retirement? Not to put a damper on all the fun and play this month, but what if you never make it there? We've all heard those stories of the hard-working person who saved their fun and dreams for after retirement, finally got there, and then...died. Of course, in this world we have to make some money, too; but maybe we don't need to save *all* of our fun and play and what we love to do for some uncertain point in the future.

So, now that we've discovered just how essential play is to our very wellbeing, it's time we re-prioritize our buckets of work and play. But before we can even begin to re-prioritize play, we have to know what it is that we actually love to do. So, ask yourself – ***what do I love to do?***

- What are the activities that naturally excite and energize me?
- What am I doing when time just seems to fly by, when I look at my watch suddenly and realize three hours have passed and I forgot to eat or pee?

- What is it that I love to do so much that I'll keep doing it endlessly and joyfully until I finally reach exhaustion?

Pay attention to all the details: when time flies by joyfully are you typically alone, or with others? Where are you, indoors or outdoors? And what is it that you're engaging in?

Write all of your answers to this question in the first section or column on your paper labeled: *what I love to do now*. Feel free to keep adding to this list throughout the month as you continue pondering and exploring!

Question #2 - What did I love to do as a child?

In Question #1 we explored what we love to do *now*, in our current timeframe, as an adult. With this second question, I'm asking you to go back into your past, back into your childhood, and recall what you loved to do as a child. If you have a hard time remembering what you loved doing as a child, here are some things that could help:

- Look at old photos from childhood to jog your memory.
- Talk to a loved one that you trusted and enjoyed spending time with when you were a child; ask them if they remember what you loved to do. Someone older than you, like a parent, grandparent, aunt/uncle, or older sibling might have clearer memories of what you used to spend your time doing.
- Close your eyes and clear your mind by taking a few deep breaths; ask your higher self or soul self to bring you a joyful memory from childhood.

> Trust any images, words, sounds or sensations that you receive and see if they help to jog any additional memories.

Write all of your answers to this question in the second section or column on your paper titled: *what I loved to do as a child*. Feel free to keep adding to this list, too, as you continue pondering and exploring throughout the month!

Question #3 - What is the golden thread?

So, as you look over these two lists you've now created – *what I love to do now* and *what I loved to do as a child* – do you see any similarities between the two, then and now? What have you always loved?

- Physical activity as a form of play? Getting a burst of adrenaline? Watching or playing sports?
- Have you always been very social and loved to play with others? Or organize others and plan events? To tell stories and make people laugh?
- Or have you always loved time alone to go into your own inner world? To read, to write, to create?
- Have you always loved playing board games and building structures?
- Or doing arts 'n crafts, making music, cooking, or decorating your space?

See if you can find the similarities – the golden thread – between what you loved to do as a child and what you love to do now, as an adult. It might be an exact match – if you've always loved reading or writing, for example. Or it might require a stretch of the imagination – if you used to love setting up your living room as various exotic locales to visit in your imagination, and today you love traveling around the world.

For me, I loved to create endless clubs, unique businesses, and well-intentioned-but-poorly-thought-out non-profits with my best friend, Nicole. One of my favorite childhood memories is of the two of us creating a Summer Carnival and later a Fall Festival for our entire neighborhood. We organized a bunch of games and had our moms drive us to the store so we could buy all the prizes and other necessities. We created a Clip-Art flyer (remember Clip-Art in the 90s?) that we distributed around our greater neighborhood area. We hired all of our siblings to work as food, game, and face-painting vendors – and made them all wear old dance recital costumes for some weird carnival flair. What I remember loving about the process was creating a vision of something that would serve people and also be fun, working with friends to carry out that vision, as well as the satisfaction of making a little money in the end.

It's fun to look back and realize what it was about this process that I loved as a child, because it's very similar to the process that I went through to start my own business as an adult. But so often, my adult brain will make it all a bad time and over-complicate the process, because that's what adult brains do. We jade what we love with big scary expectations, enormous goals, and the idea that success only comes from hard work and stress.

Until we look around at this thing we created from a sense of play and fun, and can no longer even recognize the joy in it anymore.

Or we can't locate the play and joy in our lives at all because we forgot to include it altogether, leaving it completely behind in our childhoods in lieu of becoming a responsible, practical, hard-working adult.

But it's time to un-earth the play, or bring it back altogether!

Start by writing down in your journal any golden threads you can find between what you used to love to do as a child, and what you love to do now. There are no wrong answers and no way to do this exercise wrong – you get to approach this activity with a sense of curiosity and, you guessed it, play.

Question #4 - Putting it all together: How can I infuse my life with play?

So, you've got your lists of what you love to do now, what you loved to do as a child, and any similarities or golden threads that have existed as a constant throughout your life.

This is a pretty good starting place to turn to anytime you do have some free time to fill, or for those times when you've carved out the space in your schedule for fun and play. The more you can fill your time and your life with the things on this list, the happier and more joyful you will feel.

But also, as we said earlier, if you really want to revolutionize your life, it's important to start thinking about not only how you can add back in more ways to play, but how the very building blocks of your life can be *fueled* by what feels playful.

Instead of being driven by striving, forcing, proving, stress and fear for the other half of your life – the responsible, grown up, hard-working half – wouldn't it feel better to be driven by joy?

Remember how we wondered, what if family activities felt like playtime not only for the kids, but for the adults as well? What if date night felt like play? What if exercise felt like play? What if your very job felt like play?

In this way, play becomes much more than something to do in our spare time. It becomes something with the potential to completely rearrange and transform our life and *infuse* it with passion and joy.

To complete your Ultimate Play To-Do List, add one final section titled, *how I can infuse my life with play.* And start brainstorming any steps you could take to fuel your life with the energy of play. The fun part of this is that you don't have to feel compelled to take any of these steps right now. You just get to embody the energy of play and use your imagination to envision anything you want!

Ask yourself, if I could imagine my life in any way that I wanted, what would I imagine? Would I imagine my job feeling fun and creative instead of heavy and overwhelming? Would I imagine date night feeling light and full of laughter instead of tense and filled with conversations about work and schedules? Would I imagine exercise feeling playful and being something that I actually look forward to instead of dreading it?

In a perfect world of imagination, a world filled with play and joy and fun and laughter and creativity, what would my life look like?

Create your list in whatever way feels the most fun and creative to you. You could make a linear list of steps, draw a picture, write out specific details of your vision, or create a list of words that capture how you want your life to feel.

Then, look back over this list and pick one thing – it could be a small but impactful thing like swapping your social media scrolling time for time to enjoy an item from your list of things you love to do. Or it could be a big hairy-scary thing like finally looking for that new job that utilizes more of your creative side, if that's what your soul feels called to do. Choose anything that you can commit to putting into action this month.

Remember, it doesn't have to be an enormous change to make a huge difference – as we've said many times before, sometimes it's not about changing your life, sometimes it's about changing the way you *experience* your life. How can you experience your life in a way that feels more playful and fun?

Then make a commitment to yourself by writing down:

This month, I commit to infusing my life with play and joy by: (fill in the blank)!

Enjoy your list of fun things to do! And remember to take it just as seriously, or even more seriously, as your to-do list. Afterall, it's essential to your happiness and wellbeing.

Happy October! What's on YOUR play to-do list? How will you infuse your life with play? May you unleash your creative side, find joy in playing once again, and have fun gettin' weird with it. Here's to a month filled with much frolicking, romping and merrymaking!

CHAPTER 9

November: Making Peace with Death

So...LAST SUMMER I ATTENDED my own funeral. *More on that later.* But ever since then, I've thought – we should talk more about death. I mean, we're all afraid of it on one level or another, right? We may share the more lighthearted sentiment of Groucho Marx on trying to simply avoid death: *"I intend to live forever, or die trying."*[47] Or perhaps we fully resonate with the darker feelings shared by Leo Tolstoy in *War and Peace: "Everything ends in death, everything. Death is terrible."*[48]

But what if it wasn't terrible, and what if it wasn't the absolute worst-case scenario that we spend our whole lives fearfully trying to avoid? Wouldn't it feel better to talk about why we fear it, learn that maybe we have less to fear than we thought, and face the fear head on – rather than let it endlessly control us in the background?

We met Anita Moorjani and her miraculous story of healing in Chapter 5 during the month of July. After her experience of temporarily dying, she wrote about this near-death encounter in her book *Dying to be Me: My Journey from Cancer, to Near Death, to True Healing*. Upon returning to life following this brush with death, she reported:

> *"I was no longer afraid of anything. I didn't fear illness, aging, death, loss of money, or anything. When death holds no horror, there isn't much else left to be afraid of because it's always considered the worst-case scenario. And if the worst doesn't faze you, then what else is left?"*[49]

Maybe we should trust – at least listen to! – the people who have been there, actually tasted death and returned to say – you know what? It's not that bad. In fact, it felt pretty amazing. Because what are the rest of us even basing it on? Really nothing. And yet, because there's such a stigma around speaking about death – unless you're actually at a funeral, and even then we try to avoid it – we hold off.

But there isn't any better time to discuss such dark topics than right now, in the middle of Autumn, the season that flaunts death right in our faces whether we like to think about it or not, as we're deliciously crunching on all those dead leaves. And, while we're still in Scorpio season, the astrological sign with the reputation for all things dark or taboo.

I planned it carefully – I buttered you up last month with all the joyful practices of PLAY. I wanted to fill you up with something that just *makes ya feel good*. So that this month I could carefully bomb you with the topic of death, and hopefully not lose you right away. You're welcome. But honestly, I'm just being silly and overly dramatic – because my point is actually quite the opposite.

It's not that a topic like death needs to be a bummer. It can actually help us to *feel better* about life – if we just allow ourselves to remove the topic from the darkness where it's been festering and decaying, and bring it out into the light. And by the end of this chapter, you'll have ten practices to work with – *and make peace with* – the elements of death and letting go in your own life.

Working with Death: On 3 Levels

When we think about the idea of death, I want us to think of it in relation to three different levels:

1. LETTING GO – the practice of "little deaths," as in releasing the old that no longer serves us, in order to create the space for new growth and magic in our lives. This might occur every day, once a month, every year – this is the part of death and letting go that we *can* control, and we'll feel better once we make a conscious practice out of it!

2. AUTUMN – the yearly season of dying and letting go within the greater ongoing natural cycles of nature. We can't control death at this level, but for the most part aside from some grumbles about the colder weather, we seem to make peace with it – and can engage in some super helpful practices for letting go on a deep emotional level gleaned from the wisdom of this season.

3. DEATH – what we see as the final stop, but is really just one stop on the wheel of life within the Great Cycle of life and death. We can't control this, *but we*

desperately want to. By working with the practices below, we can engage with this level of death that scares us the most, and learn to make peace with it.

Level 1 - Letting Go

A big piece of our fear of death is that it's the greatest thing in our lives that we can't control. So, before jumping in to make peace with the idea of death, start by making peace with the idea of *letting go of control* (remember those levels of "surrender" we discussed in the introduction of this book?). And before you even start making peace with letting go of control, begin by becoming comfortable with the idea of simply *letting go.*

Death on this level takes on many forms. It is the idea of shedding, releasing, letting go of what no longer serves us. As the wise teacher Lao Tzu has said: *"To attain knowledge, add things every day; to attain wisdom, remove things every day."*[50] This removing may be in the form of people, places, things. It may be giving less of our energy to draining relationships, friendships, jobs. Or removing stuff lying around our house that we no longer use.

It may be shedding limiting beliefs, old behavioral patterns, outgrown values. It may be releasing our attachment to certain roles we have outgrown, or labels that keep us feeling small. It may be letting go of what other people think, in order to better access our own inner wisdom. Or letting go of doing things that feel like they are killing our soul – even if it goes against societal ideas of what we "should" be doing.

No matter what form it takes, a "little death" at this level is always in service to the greater idea of *making space* for that which does serve us. That which lights us up, and allows us to grow and shine.

And "little" though they may be in comparison to the greater death we go through at the end of our time, a death at this level is by no means inconsequential or even easy. But the most tangible, perhaps simplest entry point to letting go on this level is at the level of our *things*. We live in a world where we're made to feel that we always need more in order to feel whole – more information, more friends, more followers, more beautiful things to fill our homes with. But we're not taught the importance of letting go of the old.

I was recently at a place personally where my closets were completely full and I was always running out of hangers. My basement was cluttered to the brim with the same ridiculous piles of *"things to go through later"* from four years ago when we first moved in. And while I do love to pretend that I'm a certain beloved red-haired mermaid singing in my underwater cave of wonders about all my neat stuff, I have enough tiny treasures to fill every surface in my office.

There's nothing wrong with having things, let's be clear. But how do the things make you feel? There can be a correlation to how we feel on an emotional level and the condition of our physical space. It's hard to say what comes first. Do we feel chaotic in our lives, and that's why we have our stuff strewn about in total disarray? Or does the disarray make us feel emotionally chaotic? Do we feel stuck or stagnant in our lives, and therefore lack the motivation to clear out our overflowing closets? Or do our stuffed closets make us feel stuck and stagnant every time we look at them?

For me, there was an *a-ha* about this sort of connection when my shamanic teacher mentioned a correlation between the levels of our house and the levels of our consciousness. For example, the basement can be linked to the subconscious as well as to emotional baggage in the past. In real life, the hubs and I kept trying to get a fresh start on our relationship dynamics and yet the ghosts of our past continued to plague us. At the same time, *"clean out basement"* was a running to-do list item for four years. Is there any correlation? Can the question of, *how do we clean out our emotional baggage from the past* become – at least partially – a matter of cleaning out all the junk sitting around in our basement?

What is the room or area of the house for you where stuff tends to endlessly accumulate? How does it make you feel when you look at it? What if you could let go of that feeling by letting go of some of that stuff? It's not a silver bullet – we're not going to solve all our problems simply by cleaning our houses. But we do have an effect on our surroundings, and our surroundings do have an effect on us. So, you can expect a shift on some level.

And as we remove the stuff that surrounds us, and remove some of the emotional stagnancy and baggage connected to that, we can start to create the space to access deeper and deeper levels of letting go. Below are four practices you can work with to engage with this energy of letting go in your own life.

Empowering Personal Practices for Letting Go & Shedding the Old

1. Clear the Physical Clutter

To shift how you feel on an emotional level. From physical clutter and emotional stagnancy – to physical space and emotional freedom. See the above section for examples.

2. Shed Soul-Killing Practices

Run a soul check-in and ask yourself: *Does this thing/role/ belief/practice/person/relationship/etc. make my soul feel expansive and empowered, or does it make me feel small, angry, or disempowered?*

Decide if it's time to completely let go of that soul-killing practice, of if you can at least start putting less of your energy into it, or change your relationship to it. This frees up space for those practices that make your soul come alive! A good time to run this soul check-in is every time you come to your Full Moon Releasing Ritual that you first learned about in Chapter 2 during the month of April.

There was a time in my life when I would hear myself say, *this such-and-such is killing my soul.* And I think what I secretly longed for was someone to say, "hey, that sounds important! Don't kill your soul!" So, I'm letting you know if you ever feel that way – *hey, that's important! And you don't have to kill your soul.* Let's find another way.

3. Let Go of What Other People Think

To make space to care about what YOU think, feel, intuit, and know. For us chronic people-pleasers this is a hard one, but it's so important. You may feel like you're dying if you're not getting the approval you crave, but if you're habitually going against what YOU feel, intuit and know to be true for yourself just to make others happy, *that's* what's going to kill you. A lack of approval can definitely hurt, but know that it's probably more about that person's own fears, worries, and self-judgements than it is about you.

Of course, you can still ask for wise counsel from your most trusted friends and advisors, but also start to trust your own wise self. When you can firmly stand by your choices and know that you're doing the right thing for yourself, you'll no longer crave that approval from others.

A good way to start gaining trust in your decisions is by learning to listen to your intuition. Revisit the Soulful Intuitive Decisions practice from Chapter 3 during the month of May to keep working on this skill!

4. *Release Attachment to Your Roles/Labels -*

To make space to be your true self. It's easy to place ourselves into comfortable roles – *mother, father, daughter, sister, teacher, accountant, manager, healer, coach.* We also place ourselves into disempowering roles – *perfectionist, people-pleaser, control-freak, anxious, depressed, sick.* In actuality, NONE of these roles are who we are.

If we get too used to being the sick person, what happens when we get healthy? Who are we now? What is our purpose? What happens when we're the mother and our children go off to college leaving us in our empty nest? Who are we now? What is our purpose?

My shamanic teacher says that when she introduces herself even in a professional capacity, she doesn't say, *Hi I'm Amy and I'm a teacher, healer, and shaman* – she just says *Hi, I'm Amy.* So, hold all of your roles and labels gently off to the side as something you can step into and out of fluidly as needed. And instead, step fully into being YOU, in all of your glory, with all of your flaws and perfect imperfections, with all of your many facets and talents, with everything that you're working on and everything that you already are.

Know that you are enough, and know that your greatest purpose is to be more and more of your true authentic self. Enjoy meeting the person underneath all those roles and labels. And let's try this: *Hi, I'm Angela. Who are you?*

Level 2 - Autumn

Death on this level is our yearly reminder that all things change – and are meant to. It's our reminder that in the cycle of life there is always death, and through death new life is brought forth. As we watch the leaves fall from the trees, we can find comfort in knowing that we don't actually have to try so hard to control everything, because it is all flowing along in grander cycles according to a plan larger than us.

It's a good time to take a seasonal inventory of your life in order to complete a series of "little deaths" in your own life, as outlined in all the suggested practices in the last section for letting go and shedding the old. Because although it can be helpful to always carry a spirit of letting go with us throughout the whole year, I find that Autumn and Scorpio season bring it to a whole new level of depth. There's something about this time of year that always seems to pull the skeletons out of the closet, seems to dredge up the darkness hiding out in our shadows.

And we can either resist that, keeping its power over us, allowing this old programming to run our lives unconsciously from the shadows...or we can work with it, and bring it out into the light. Even though it can be uncomfortable or painful to do so, it's the only way we can transform these old, dark, outdated parts of ourselves into more wholeness, or release them altogether to free up more space for living as our true authentic selves.

In Chinese Medicine, Autumn is also associated with the organs of the Lungs and the Large Intestine. The Large Intestine is a major organ of elimination, clearing out the waste products that no longer serve us. The Lungs draw in the pure, the new, the very breath that replenishes and cleanses us. These two organs work together energetically, in harmony – to clear out the old, and welcome in the new.

When our Large Intestine energy is balanced, we may enjoy smooth and effortless digestion, organized thinking and ease in decision making, as well as a sense of flow in life, especially in relation to money and relationships. But when out of balance, we may experience digestive ailments, skin issues, sore throats and stuffed sinuses, toothaches, or chronic pain in the arm and shoulder. We may find we have cloudy thinking and impaired decision making. We may feel stubborn, angry or resentful in relationships. And instead of a healthy sense of flow and letting go, we may discover we are hoarding resources or holding in emotions like grief.

While an imbalance of blocked or stagnant energy in the Large Intestine energy channel can be an underlying factor in the ailments listed above, keep in mind that living our lives in this way in an extended manner – experiencing ongoing anger or resentment in our relationships, or holding in deep emotions like grief – can also *be* the contributing factor to creating an imbalance in Large Intestine energy, which can then lead to the ailments listed above.

It's the age-old question again, which came first? But the influence can go both ways, keeping us locked in these unhealthy patterns. Maybe you find yourself experiencing some of these ailments listed above and desperately want to break the cycle, or maybe you just want to support your overall health and wellbeing at this time of year. Either way, an excellent practice that stems from the wisdom of Autumn is the practice of deeply letting go. We see the trees do it every year, completing a cycle of death in order to be birthed anew in the spring – and we can, too. You can use the two practices listed below to engage with this even deeper level of emotional letting go in your own life.

Autumn-Inspired Practices for Letting Go & Deep Emotional Cleansing

1. Address Anger & Resentment in Relationships

To remove the strain on your Large Intestine chi/energy. Easier said than done, but the first step is awareness. If you're not allowing yourself to be aware of the anger and resentment within you, then you're giving your power away to it and letting *it* control *you.*

There's a social stigma around experiencing or expressing anger, especially for women. But interestingly, a certain level of resentment seems socially acceptable in relationships, so it's quite common for anger to exist in its less obvious form of slow-simmering, just-below-the-surface resentment. Sometimes we don't even realize it's there as we've gotten so used to the feeling.

But know that it's more than ok to feel anger. The feeling is completely natural and it's important to express it, although there are ways we can learn to do this that are healthier and more skillful than others. And while it might be common to feel resentment, it isn't necessary, it can be healed, and it's only hurting you in the meantime.

As you get into deeper layers of this healing process, you might also find that the guidance of a trusted professional is helpful, such as a therapist or coach specializing in boundary setting or relationships. The grief practice below can also work in tandem with the practice of dissolving resentments, so be sure to explore that as well.

Be kind to yourself by noticing if these feelings are present and deciding that you want to do something about it. Oftentimes anger and resentment are present because there's a need going unmet. Ask yourself, *what need is going unmet for me?* And then listen gently and intently to the answer that speaks from your soul.

2. Allow Grief to Flow

To remove the strain on your Lung and Large Intestine chi/energy. So often we keep grief locked away, wreaking havoc on our bodies. Find a safe space, maybe alone or with a trusted companion or journal, and allow the tears/anger/grief/sadness to flow. Know that this is one of the most natural, healing, and cleansing things you can do for yourself physically, emotionally, and energetically. As author and dreamworker Toko-pa Turner says in her book *Belonging: Remembering Ourselves Home,*

> *"Grief plays an essential role in our coming undone from previous attachments. It is the necessary current we need to carry us into our next becoming. Without it, we may remain stuck in that area of our life, which can limit the whole spectrum of our feeling alive."*

She goes on to say with exquisite eloquence,

> *"Grief is the expression of healing in motion. As you make the seemingly bottomless descent, it helps to remember that grief is the downpour your soul has been thirsting for."*[51]

We cannot become our truest, brightest, and most authentic selves if we are weighed down and shackled by heavy burdens from the past. What have you not grieved? We grieve for all sorts of endings – when we lose someone we've loved, from death but also through the ending of relationships with lovers, friends, family. We grieve for who we once were – when something big sweeps in and changes our whole perception of ourselves, like illness or an accident or the loss of a career that shaped our whole identity.

We grieve for our child-self and all the little-t and big-T traumas that we had to endure as an innocent being unable to properly process these experiences. As adults, we eventually do the grieving for that inner child. We grieve when we need to forgive – others as well as ourselves. It can feel like all we have to hold on to for protection is our anger and our resentment, but to forgive means to let go of that anger, and the only thing to wash it away is the deluge of our deep sadness from our broken hearts.

As we complete this cycle around the wheel of the year, this is our darkest stop. This is the time to dig deep, to face our greatest fears and do our greatest healing work in service to our personal evolution. It's not easy, and it's not comfortable, but you can do it. While we don't know what will kill us, I can assure you that this work won't be the thing to kill you, though we may fear it will be so.

As mentioned in the previous section, this sort of healing work may be best suited for the guidance of a trusted professional like a therapist, coach, healer or shaman who specializes in griefwork, trauma, and deep healing. Know what's right for you, and where and when you need extra support.

We must remember that the path to true and lasting health and happiness is not for the faint of heart. But if you feel this particular yearning inside of you, you know there is no other option. You are a fierce warrior, a great explorer, a leader with a vision. You are a gentle soul, a sensitive being, a child that just wants to be heard. They say the only way is through and you know this to be true. Walls will fall, defenses will fail, distance will not serve you now. Into the heart of the beast you go, and there is only one way you will emerge the other side: *victorious*.

BONUS – While working on emotional releasing work at these deep levels, know that the practices of Yin Yoga, acupressure and acupuncture can also be especially supportive because of their ability to balance our meridians, or energy channels. You can use these practices as additional tools to help support and clear your Large Intestine and Lung energy channels at the same time that you're doing the deep personal work above to decrease the overall negative strain on them.

Level 3 - Death

As I mentioned at the beginning of this chapter, last summer I attended my own funeral. That may sound funny, seeing as how I am still alive and well – but it was quite an eye-opening experience. You may be thinking of that *Friends* episode where Ross throws himself a funeral just to see if anybody really cares, and is so pleased by the nice things that people are saying about him that he jumps out from his hiding spot in the corner, sure that everyone will be delighted. The surprise doesn't go over so well.[52] So, don't go about it that way – we shouldn't have to actually fake our own deaths just to hear the nice things people have to say about us!

My "funeral" was part of the shamanic training program that I went through. It was our first week where I barely knew these people who were now standing huddled around my body, lying on a massage table where I was doing my best version of playing dead. Someone had just read the eulogy I'd written for the occasion, and now everyone was taking a turn remembering a funny or heartwarming memory from the last three days or saying what they liked or admired about me.

It was actually quite lovely and I barely knew these people. Imagine doing this with those you've known your whole life! If you're looking to shake up your family Thanksgiving ritual of going around the table and saying what you're grateful for...have each person play dead while the rest shower them with nice things. I'm kidding, but also not kidding. Consider some version of it! Don't save all the nice things to say about each other for after that person is gone. Consider what you could share with them now, while they're still here.

About a year later, back at my shamanic training, I found myself once again lying on a massage table playing dead. This time I wasn't dead yet, but practicing those moments on our deathbed just before we cross over. The most impactful part of this experience was the deathbed conversations I had with individuals playing my family members, as well as my experience playing other people's family members and having tearful conversations with the almost departed.

Just like we tend to save all the great things we have to say about people until after they're gone, what else do we tend to save for the end of our lives? All the hard things we want to say, the repairs and the amends. It's actually lucky if we even do get the chance to make these repairs and amends on our deathbed, because it's just as likely we could pass unexpectedly. But just like we don't have to save all the nice things we have to say, we also don't have to save all the hard things we want to say. We can choose right now to make the repairs and the amends – either with the person, written to the person, or written into our journal if that person isn't alive anymore, or if it would be unwise or unsafe to reconnect with them.

Having unfinished business can keep our soul tethered to this realm after we cross over. If you can finish that business now, you can free your soul to be fully released to the light on the other side. This is letting go on a whole other level. These aren't easy things, because saying the nice things and saying the hard things can feel extremely vulnerable – but they are do-able things. And it's nice to know we have options to make peace with these practices now, instead of having to wait for the surprise of death to determine when we do them.

You can use the four practices listed below to start engaging with this deepest level of letting go – the level of death itself – in your own life. Start making peace with death, and you'll find that feeling better about death is a sure portal to feeling better about life.

Conscious Practices to Engage with the Great Cycle of Life & Death

1. *Write Your Eulogy*

Writing it as though you died today, what would it say? What character traits would it include? What great accomplishments? What challenges or hardships that you persevered through? What funny or touching stories?

Write it out, and then reflect – are you satisfied with how your life has gone? Do you have any regrets? Unaccomplished goals? Unrealized dreams? Is something missing?

Allow that to inspire you on your path as you take your next steps. Knowing that you likely aren't dying today as you write your eulogy, take comfort in knowing that you still have time to influence your course of events.

What is still inside of you that aches to come out? What creations, what achievements, what steps of personal growth? As journalist Norman Cousins has famously observed, *"Death is not the greatest loss in life. The greatest loss is what dies inside us while we live."*[53] Begin taking steps to let this out!

2. *Share the Nice Things with Others*

Instead of saving it for after they are gone. As mentioned above, this could become your new Thanksgiving practice. You don't have to take it to the same degree that I did at my training, lying on a bed and having everyone surround the body – unless you want to get extra weird and dark with your Thanksgiving rituals, in which case I fully support you!

For example, my own family took inspiration from this idea last year and made up our own version of the practice. We turned it into a bit of a fun craft project, too. Each person stapled a few sheets of lined paper onto a colorful sheet of construction paper, wrote their name at the top, and then listed everyone else's names down the side of the lined paper leaving a few blank lines between each name. Then we decorated our papers with a slew of fun and sparkly stickers.

Throughout the course of the evening, everyone had a chance to write something nice about each person on their paper, at their leisure. Then, the next time we all gathered, we took turns reading out loud all the nice things written on our papers. It was a really touching and fun experience, and something we're already thinking about instituting on a possible yearly basis! And the benefit of having it written down is that you can come back to it anytime you need a little pick me up.

In case you're thinking this is a practice only for the adults, we did this with our whole group, ages 13 to 70! And I think it would work just fine for younger kids, too. It's up to you how you'd want to phrase it and explain *why* you're doing it, but the sooner you can start to not fear death and instead make peace with it, the better, in my opinion.

3. *Life Review & Deathbed Convos*

Review your life from the moment you were born up until this very moment. Usually, we see our life from the perspective of how everything has made *us* feel; but in this case, review your life from the perspective of *everyone you may have negatively affected.*

Then make the repairs and amends now. You can do so directly, with that person, or in writing to the person. Or indirectly, without that person present, but instead with a trusted companion willing to simply listen and witness without any judgment, or in your journal between you and your soul. As mentioned earlier, you don't have to make the amends in person if you feel it would be unwise or unsafe to reconnect with the person, or if they aren't alive anymore, or if you're simply not ready to and want to work your way up to that.

The goal doesn't have to be about repairing relationships – it certainly might be, but that might not feel like the best route to take depending on the situation. It can also simply be about tying up unfinished business – like strong emotions towards a person or situation that haven't been fully processed yet – that could keep your soul tethered here instead of free to move on.

Take steps now to acknowledge the hard things, and seize this opportunity to tie up your loose ends.

4. *Create an Altar*

For those loved ones that have already passed. This might include photos, objects that remind you of that person, sacred items like healing stones, or anything that feels special and right. Talk to your loved ones that have passed – out loud, to your altar, in your journal, or in your mind while you're trying to fall asleep. The altar, and the talking to them, are ways to keep your connection alive. And who knows, they just might still be able to hear you.

BONUS 1 – Read about near-death experiences (NDEs) and expose yourself to the possibilities of life after death.

BONUS 2 – Listen to *On Death, Autumn & Letting Go*, a playlist on Spotify that my musichead husband and I created, and allow yourself to process this topic on a level that's even deeper than the mind, by *feeling* about it instead. Because our experience of music is so tied to our emotions, it can sometimes be an even more effective way to process something that's challenging. And feeling our way through death is no exception. You can find the playlist on Spotify by searching for "On Death, Autumn & Letting Go" and/or my username: moondancing. Turn it on, lie on the ground, and let it wash over you. May this musical playlist serve as a comforting friend for the hard times.

-NOVEMBER PRACTICE-

TEN BIZARRE RITUALS:
FEEL BETTER ABOUT DEATH TO FEEL
BETTER ABOUT LIFE

No exploration of the fall would be complete without a dive into the realm of darkness. This month, you'll gain a list of ten bizarre rituals to start engaging with – and making peace with – the elements of death and letting go in your own life.

You have now been exposed to ten practices and bizarre rituals for working with *and making peace with* the elements of death and letting go in your own life. One way you could decide how to get started is by choosing one practice from each of the three categories – Letting Go, Autumn, and Death – to engage with this month. Feel free to engage with more than that, but as a general rule, this journey isn't about trying to do ALL the things ALL at once; it's about doing less, slowly and sustainably. So, aim to do one thing really well, instead of overwhelming yourself trying to do everything.

Maybe there's a couple practices you feel excited or curious about, or maybe there's one big one that you know will take all of your time and energy and you want to put all of your focus there. There aren't any rules, just ideas to get you started. In the end, it's up to YOU. There's no right or wrong way to go about this when deciding which practices to choose. See what piques your curiosity or resonates with you the most and start there.

All 10 practices are listed again below, by category, and the descriptions for each can be found on the previous few pages. Stay curious, allow it to be fun when it can be fun, allow it to be challenging and uncomfortable when it needs to be challenging and uncomfortable. Allow yourself to see what unfolds. May you be delighted and transformed by choosing to consciously engage with these practices!

Level 1: Letting Go

Empowering Personal Practices for Letting Go & Shedding the Old (see pages 210-214)

1.   *Clear the Physical Clutter*
2.   *Shed Soul-Killing Practices*
3.   *Let Go of What Other People Think*
4.   *Release Attachment to Your Roles/Labels*

Level 2: Autumn

Autumn-Inspired Practices for Letting Go & Deep Emotional Cleansing (see pages 215-220)

1.   *Address Anger and Resentment in Relationships*
2.   *Allow Grief to Flow*

BONUS: *Yin yoga, acupressure, acupuncture in conjunction with the above.*

Level 3: Death

Conscious Practices to Engage with the Great Cycle of Life & Death (see pages 220-225)

1. *Write Your Eulogy*
2. *Share the Nice Things with Others*
3. *Life Review & Deathbed Convos*
4. *Create an Altar*

BONUS: *Read about NDEs*

BONUS: *Listen to the Music, Death & Letting Go playlist*

How will you integrate the practices of death and letting go into YOUR life this month? From the practical work of cleaning out your home, to the deep inner work of emotional letting go; from shedding the behaviors that no longer serve you, to reflecting on your life up to this point and making your amends – may you enjoy experimenting with these 10 practices listed above. And in so doing, may you find some peace with the circle of life and death.

PART IV

WINTER

Winter Intro:
Deep Rest & Reset

WELCOME TO WINTER. A season defined in nature by quiet, stillness, and the pause before the new growth that will follow in the spring. But how do we define it in our own human lives? Do we, too, allow ourselves any sense of pause, of quiet, of slowness or stillness? Or do we push on through, determined that winter should feel exactly like every other season. There is something our wily human minds miss that every other species alive on this earth seems to intuitively understand: winter is a time for rest.

This is a season of *"full yin"* energy. Where summer was our time of "full yang" energy, a time of going and doing and socializing, of brightness and light and heat and outward facing energy – winter is the exact opposite. This is the time of turning our focus inward and exploring our inner world rather than the world around us. It's a time for reflection and introspection; for spending time in our cozy abode hibernating with our loved ones; for deep rest and rejuvenation; for darkness and stillness and quiet.

But because we are always seeking equilibrium, we must attend to the balance we need in this season, as well. Most of us in our American culture – despite whatever yin or yang season it is – need more yin energy in our lives, because we're skewed so heavily in the opposite yang direction. But winter can also become dark, and cold, and monotonous, and we may find ourselves falling out of balance in the direction of yin – becoming depressed, lethargic, or uninspired.

So, in the month of December, we'll explore a way to keep our inner fire and spark alive throughout this season by playing around with the practice of dance! Not a dance practice that comes from any externally choreographed steps, but one that unites you with the creative inspiration of your own soul and spirit.

Then in January, when we greet the new calendar year, we'll find a way to honor these new beginnings, but in a way that is more in alignment with the energy of the winter season. Instead of setting resolutions and trying to *force* and *make* them happen, we'll explore two quiet, reflective ways for you to create a powerful vision for the year ahead.

And finally in February where our journey ends, we'll explore how going into the cocoon – slowing down, turning inward, becoming still and quiet – is actually the perfect, and necessary, conditions for new life to spring forth as we ready ourselves for the journey to begin once again. You'll have a chance to engage in some reflection on the journey you've just completed, *and* you'll get to do a little celebrating of how far you've come in a very cozy, hygge way!

May you enjoy a new experience of the winter season this year, one that encourages you to fully steep yourself in the nourishing, soul-soothing elements of this season as intended by nature, and that allows you to emerge into spring refreshed and re-balanced!

CHAPTER 10

December:
Dance Medicine

THIS MONTH IN THE NORTHERN hemisphere, we will experience the Winter Solstice. Typically occurring on Dec 21 or 22, this marks the official start of the winter season. For the last six months following the Summer Solstice in June, the days have slowly been getting shorter and the nights getting longer. The change is imperceptible at first, until we reach this darkest time of the year, marked by the darkest day with the shortest period of daylight and the longest period of nighttime. But not only is the Winter Solstice the darkest day of the year – it is also the herald of light. Following the solstice, the days will once again slowly begin to lengthen all the way until the Summer Solstice, when we experience the longest, lightest day of the year in mid-June.

The Solstice: A Cross-Cultural Celebration

The Winter Solstice has been celebrated across cultures since the beginning of time. Fires, feasts, candles, rituals, dancing – have been seen as ways to keep spirits high during a cold and dark time, to ward off illness and evil spirits, and to bolster people with feelings of hope and resilience as they celebrate the return of the sun and the light.

As new religions sprung up over time, including Christianity, many old and new traditions started to fuse with one another as this was already seen as a sacred and festive time. Often synonymous with Christmas, Yule is one of the oldest solstice celebrations around. Ancient Nordic peoples celebrated Yule, beginning on the Winter Solstice, when a large log – the yule log – would burn for twelve days while the people feasted, drank, sang carols, and danced.

Long ago, the Romans celebrated Saturnalia, a week-long festival for the god of agriculture – Saturn – leading up to the Winter Solstice. It was a time of feasting, drinking, festivities – and a unique tradition that turned the social hierarchy upside down where masters would wait on their servants and enslaved people were temporarily granted freedom and treated as equals.

The Iranian festival of Yalda is still celebrated today with its roots in ancient times celebrating the birth of the Persian Sun God, Mithra. Family gatherings, feasts, candles and fires lit all night would celebrate the victory of light over dark.

Dong Zhi is an important festival in China celebrated thousands of years ago as well as today with families gathering to make rice wine, dumplings, and celebrate the balancing forces of yin and yang with the coming arrival of the light to soon balance out the abundance of dark.

For the Native American Hopi tribe of northern Arizona, Soyal is the Winter Solstice celebration that includes rituals for purification, gift-giving, and dancing. It is a time to ceremonially welcome the sun back from its long slumber and invite in protective spirits from the mountains.

The Zuni people of western New Mexico see the Winter Solstice as the beginning of the new year. For them it is marked with a ceremonial dance called Shalako. After several days of dancing, ceremony, and prayers, new dancers are chosen for the coming year, and the cycle of the new year then begins again.

Stoking our Inner Fire

As a child in Minnesota, I remember celebrating the Winter Solstice by decorating myself with plastic flower leis and dancing to festive music in the living room. Fast forward a few decades later when I celebrated a recent Winter Solstice with another kind of dancing ritual. I attended a three-hour *Qoya Inspired Movement* class, a style of dance that is rooted in authentic freeform movement, yoga, and shamanic practices. The founder of Qoya, Rochelle Schieck, explains that the main goal of a Qoya class is to remind ourselves that our true essence is *wise, wild, and free* – and to express this through our movement.[54]

It was the exact medicine that I needed at this time of year. Both the hubs and I had just had the flu a few weeks prior to that, and even though the main symptoms had resolved, the post-viral syndrome – fatigue, weakness, depression – continued to hang on to both of us. Reluctantly returning to my calendar and to-do lists, I wondered what person had enthusiastically planned all these new projects for the new year that I was now looking at with very little interest or motivation. I suspected that a person with much more energy and excitement had once lived inside of me, but I couldn't locate her at that moment.

Had I not already invested in the upcoming Qoya workshop, I knew that I would have found many an excuse to avoid dragging myself out of the house in the cold and dark for three hours of dancing. Like trying to convince ourselves to sit and meditate when our lives are the most chaotic, it's funny how it can be such a challenge to give to ourselves what we need the most. Thankfully my monetary investment got my butt out the door and I arrived at a class perfectly entitled, *"Ignite the Light Within."* I set my intention for that day's class as: *today I'm dancing to return to life.*

Long enjoyed as part of Winter Solstice traditions across time and culture, I experienced on that day how dancing can truly be the medicine we need to shift our energy at this low-energy time of year. I left that class feeling renewed, alive. Whether or not we choose to celebrate the solstice with lit candles and fires burning all night, we can certainly use dancing as a way to keep our own *inner* fire stoked and our inner light alive throughout this darkest time of the year.

Dancing and Freedom

My own relationship to dancing is long and varied. I officially remember it beginning in kindergarten when I signed up for community dance classes with my best friend, Nicole. I still remember some of the moves from my first recital as a five-year-old, dancing to the 1960s Lesley Gore song *"It's My Party"* lamenting the woes of teenage love.[55] I continued on with various styles of choreographed dance – ballet, tap, jazz, modern, hip-hop – all the way through college. Outside of choreographed dance, I always loved going to dance clubs as a twenty-something. You have a couple drinks, lose that pesky self-consciousness and happily dance with all the other uninhibited young folks.

Interestingly, choreographed dancing and alcohol-induced dancing have something in common – both of them are ways to move our body, yet we can easily do either without really being *present* to the experience, or *present* to ourselves. In choreography, someone tells you to move your body this way and so you do. But it's not the same as allowing the movement to emerge from *within* you. It's an outside-in decision, rather than an inside-out inspiration.

And at a club or party, you might drink to lose the self-consciousness that keeps you from dancing freely, but along with your inhibition leaving, so does a part of the real you. I do think that mind-altering substances can play a role in exposing us to a version of ourselves that exists without all the heavy layers of conditioned fear and expectations, the woundedness, the self-consciousness. Used in the right context, psychoactive substances can be ceremonial, they can be fun, they can be healing.

But it can also become a way to keep running away from all of those heavy layers of false-self *without* doing the work to heal it. There might be a free-er, wilder, more joyful version of ourselves that lives underneath all those heavy layers, but how free are we really if we have to rely on a substance outside of ourselves as the only reliable way to get us there?

I distinctly remember an experience more recently, standing in a nightclub at a concert of The Midnight, when I *wanted* to dance – but I looked around at all the other stoic Midwesterners standing completely still, bopping only their heads to the music, and I felt that familiar rush of self-consciousness and fear. Instead of dancing because *I desired to*, I was frozen in socially-conforming behavior I didn't even want to be frozen in. Without enough liquid courage to drop my defenses, I just stood there, bopping my head. I felt envious of the few confident souls who were blissfully dancing away, and it was in that moment that I thought, I'm so tired of this self-consciousness. Who's really in control here, *me or the fear?* And I thought, I want to heal that. I want to be *truly free.*

From 'Fun Experience' to Healing Medicine

The decision to name my wellness coaching business "*Moondance*" was actually inspired by my very first encounter with a shaman, years before I would ever consider doing any shamanic training myself. I met this shamanic practitioner while living in Milwaukee, Wisconsin, of all the mystical places in the world. We met through an acquaintance, but I then sought help from her to heal from Crohn's disease and the many intestinal surgeries I had just undergone. During our session, she told me that I had a lot of *"moon energy,"* and that my legs were energetically bound and I needed to dance. Though I've danced my entire life in one form or another, I told her I was trying to let that go as a hobby and looking for a new adult hobby. I'll never forget how she advised me, *"that would be a very bad idea."*

So, I vowed then that I wouldn't let dancing go completely and continued to seek out classes and opportunities to dance, although it often seemed harder to find as an adult. And even when I named my business Moondance, I still didn't really think of dancing as being a tool for healing in any literal sense. The name was meant to refer more to the figurative, metaphorical dance of life –

how we interact with and integrate our own moon, or yin, energy; how our spirit dances with life itself. But I've come full circle to acknowledge that while there is the metaphorical dance of life, there is also the very literal dance of the body – and the heart, and soul and spirit. And both are important to consider!

I found that throughout my own shamanic training that I eventually underwent, I kept feeling the pull back towards dancing in the literal sense, and finally came to see it as a necessary tool of healing. Something that was necessary for my own personal path of healing – as that shaman six years prior had once advised me – as well as something to bring to others to support their healing.

It was due to two experiences that I had in 2022 at the tail-end of the pandemic that I fully realized the magic and power of dance to truly connect us with our soul and spirit. At a Celtic shaman training in Green Bay, Wisconsin, one of the very last things we did was dance. Before dancing, we laid on the ground and the teacher, Amantha Murphy, guided us on a shamanic journey to meet our animal helpers and allies. Then we got up, put a blindfold over our eyes, and while Amantha drummed out a beat, we danced *as* our animal companions.

With all of us blindfolded and doing our own thing, I felt the freedom in what the poet Rumi once advised: *"dance like no one is watching."*[56] I slithered my body side to side like a snake, crept low like a jaguar, reached up to the sky like a bear on its hind legs, soared like an eagle with my arms out wide and narrowly escaped taking out a few people. During all of this, I could have sworn I was still in the same general corner of the room where I had started dancing. Which is why I was so bewildered and amazed when we finally sat down and took off our blindfolds...to find that I was halfway across the big room, kitty corner from where I had begun.

Without the ability to over-focus on the experience happening outside of myself – where my attention often is, tied up in thinking about other people, and their experience, and their experience of experiencing me...I had been able to completely focus on the internal experience happening inside of myself. And I felt – ecstatic! Which the Oxford Languages dictionary officially defines as: *"overwhelming happiness or joyful excitement."*[57] Sometimes referred to as "conscious dance," I now understood why this particular method of freestyle movement is also called *"ecstatic dance."*

Leaving the training that day, completely sweaty and joyful, I drove the four hours back home and mulled over the experience, determined to find it again. Which I did, about a month later, with my friend Lauren in Boulder, Colorado. After finishing an extremely intense and fulfilling week of working on and completing a huge work project together, we treated ourselves to an evening of ecstatic dance with a local group. This time our eyes weren't blindfolded; they were wide open. The only rules at such an event are: no substances, and no talking on the dance floor. It's even discouraged to dance *with* anyone else. Instead, the intention is an opportunity to dance with yourself – to see what arises within you emotionally, and to express that inside-out through your movement. Anything goes and there's a feeling of no judgement, as everyone is there for the same experience. To dance freely with yourself. To be fully present to the experience and present to whatever arises, however uncomfortable – or joyous! – that might be.

For me, the experience of leaving an ecstatic or "conscious" dance is completely different from the experience of leaving a choreographed dance class or a dance club. While a professional dancer knows that it is possible to incorporate your emotions into a choreographed dance class – and even encouraged and necessary in order for dance to become art – what many of us discover is that it's also possible to stay completely up in your head, trying to get the steps just right, focusing on how it looks in the mirror instead of how it feels in your body, and possibly even criticizing yourself for not doing it correctly. I know I've been there. I've even seen people leave in the middle of dance classes because they didn't feel like they were doing it *"right."* And when we're leaving a dance club, we might feel joyous and free, but we might also be half in the bag – not exactly present to the experience, present to ourselves, present to our emotions. I've been there, too.

Don't get me wrong, I think any experience of dance can be a good thing. And *your* experience with dancing might be completely different from mine. But for me, some of those experiences started to feel like more of a shiny façade that in the end, was a bit...empty. When we take these experiences and fill them instead with our soul and our spirit – it becomes something else entirely! It then transforms dance from a "fun experience," into a *healing medicine.*

Dancing has existed almost as long as human civilization itself. Across time and culture, it has served as a way to bring people together for socializing and bonding, to celebrate and entertain, and as part of cultural ceremony and religious ritual. But it has also provided a tool for people to express themselves and explore their emotions, and has been used for purposes of healing the body, heart, mind, soul, and spirit. Gabrielle Roth, the pioneering founder of the 5Rhythms movement-meditation-dance practice created in the 1970s has famously said of the ancient healing role of dance:

"In many shamanic societies, if you came to a medicine person complaining of being disheartened, dispirited or depressed, they would ask one of four questions: When did you stop dancing? When did you stop singing? When did you stop being enchanted by stories? When did you stop finding comfort in the sweet territory of silence? Where we have stopped dancing, singing, being enchanted by stories, or finding comfort in silence is where we have experienced the loss of soul. Dancing, singing, storytelling, and silence are the four universal healing salves."[58]

Ask yourself, when did *you* stop dancing?

Remembering What We Intrinsically Know

I think our relationship with dance starts way before we make our way into our first dance club, and even before we step foot into our first dance class. Have you ever turned music on around a toddler? They just naturally start bopping around, completely free, tuned in to the experience, and giving exactly zero fucks about what anyone thinks of them. We come into this world intrinsically knowing how to dance.

So, what happens? Where does that natural inclination go? Why do so many adults when asked if they like to dance answer: *"well, yes...but only if there's some alcohol involved."* And why is it often much more comfortable to step foot into a choreographed dance class than to dance without any pre-determined steps, expressing solely from the heart and soul? *Because it feels super vulnerable, right?* Especially if we didn't grow up in a culture where dancing was just an inherent part of the social fabric. Without that framework, we grow up and start to feel self-conscious, silly, vulnerable when it comes to dancing from our hearts just because we feel like it. Because we watched our elders act this way. And our own children watch us, and learn that this is what it means to be a respectable adult – it means we stop dancing for the pure joy of it.

And it starts to feel too vulnerable to share ourselves in this way, because some part of us knows that dancing is a direct expression of our heart and soul and spirit. As legendary dancer and choreographer Martha Graham has said, *"Dance is the hidden language of the soul."*[59] And how many of us walk around freely sharing our soul – that truest, most authentic expression of ourselves – with our loved ones, let alone with strangers? How many of us even expose that truest part of ourselves – to ourself?

What feelings or fears does dancing bring up for *you?* Did you grow up in a culture where it was encouraged and woven into the fabric of life? Or was it something foreign, lost as you grew up, now connected to self-consciousness and feeling silly and vulnerable? When you do dance, do you feel yourself fully in your body, expressing from your heart, or do you find yourself purely in your head – analyzing, criticizing, comparing? What if you could remember once again what it felt like to dance with as much freedom as a toddler?

Dancing, Singing, Laughing, Weeping - These Are Spiritual Practices

From a scientific perspective, one of the reasons we feel so good when we dance is that it releases chemicals in the body that make us happy. Much like all exercise, feel-good dopamine, mood-stabilizing serotonin, and pain-relieving, euphoria-inducing endorphins are all released when we dance. But it's also so much deeper than this. Dance has the power to be a healing balm, a powerful tool to help move us through challenging emotions. Of this experience, 13th-century Persian poet Rumi has said: *"Dance when you're broken open. Dance and become free."*[60] Meaning, dancing isn't just a well-earned reward or something we do solely in celebration after the hard times are over. Dancing is the medicine *for* these very times, a vehicle with which to navigate and move through them.

It is our God-given right to move; it connects us to our soul, our spirit, our divinity. Dancing, singing, laughing, weeping – these are spiritual practices; they connect us to our sense of being alive. When we don't engage in these practices, we cut ourselves off from the deepest experience of ourself: our heart, our soul, and our spirit. When we truly dance, we feel ourselves connected to something greater than our physicality. We have the opportunity to experience a profound feeling of being connected to everyone and a part of everything – including a connection to the Universe, the Divine, the Great Mystery, God.

Dancing also reconnects us to the Divine Feminine energy that lives inside all of us regardless of gender, but all too often becomes overrun by our abundant masculine/yang energy. While our Sacred Masculine energy also plays a vital role in our lives, when out of balance it can cause us to overwork our bodies, overwhelm our minds, and override our emotions. Unbalanced, it pushes us to continuously strive, and to live solely from our rational mind, disconnected from our emotions, our intuition, our creativity and self-expression. Dancing reconnects us to the Wild Woman archetype, the Queen archetype, our inner Goddess energy. The Wild Woman dances to reclaim her free, empowered essence, and she intuitively knows when she dances that she is engaging in powerful soul medicine.

Dance is healing, it is playful, it is empowering. It is a path of self-discovery – pushing us to move through deeper and deeper layers of not-self in order to unleash our true essence into the world. As influential dancer and choreographer Agnes de Mille has proclaimed: *"To dance is to be out of yourself. Larger, more beautiful, more powerful."*[61]

So...
Dance to feel.
Dance to laugh and to play.
Dance to remember who you are, to remember your inherent freedom.
Dance to be in connection to everyone and everything.
Dance to heal yourself, and your world.

-DECEMBER PRACTICE-

DANCE LIKE NO ONE IS WATCHING

As the temperatures drop outside, explore a way to keep your inner fire and spark alive by playing around with the practice of dance! Not a dance practice that comes from any externally choreographed steps, but one that unites you with the creative inspiration of your own soul and spirit.

How can you start dancing again right now?

If it feels intuitive to you, you have full permission to get up and move your body! If you're not quite sure where to start, follow the steps below for inspiration. And if you're feeling self-conscious, silly, or vulnerable – remember this Japanese proverb:

> *"We're fools whether we dance or not,*
> *so we might as well dance."[62]*

Step 1: Give yourself permission.

At that recent Qoya Inspired Movement dance class I attended, I talked to another participant about how interesting it is that everyone appeared to feel completely comfortable in this kind of un-choreographed, move-from-your-heart kind of space. She said for her, there's always someone else there dancing wildly and freely enough that it gives *her* permission to do the same. And I thought, yes! Thank god there are others here to give *me* that permission.

But then I realized that instead of having to rely on permission from someone else, I wanted to BE one of those people that gives permission to others – to encourage others to express their true, unedited, uninhibited selves. But that kind of self-empowerment begins with first giving permission to *yourself* to express *your* true, unedited, uninhibited self.

So, give *yourself* permission.

Step 2: Go solo.

Find somewhere where you can be alone, shut the blinds, close the door. You can dance *like* no one is watching, or you can create the space where that's actually true until you start to feel more comfortable.

Step 3: Create a sacred space.

You can do this in a lot of ways – light a candle, burn some herbs or incense, say a prayer, ring a bell, pull an oracle card. Whatever feels special and right to you to help set the stage for this to be a healing experience.

You could also choose to start by meditatively sipping a cup of heart-opening cacao or calming tea. The theobromine found in chocolate and the L-theanine in tea (found only in true tea: green/black/white/oolong/puerh) can have soothing, mood-enhancing effects on the body and mind that help put you in the right state of mind – or, *heart* – to dance. But skip any other substances to make this a truly healing experience.

Step 4: Choose music that you love.

Any genre, any mood, upbeat or slow, whatever inspires you in that moment. I've made some playlists that can help get you started if you're not sure where to begin! You can find them on Spotify by searching the names of these lists and/or my username: *moondancing*.

1. MOVE YOUR FEET (*dance-y grooves to make you move*)

2. A RAY OF SUNSHINE (*explore a more diverse array of feels*)

3. MOONDANCING (*perfect for your next full moon dance sesh*)

Step 5: Drop awareness into the heart.

Close your eyes, breathe deeply and slowly in through the nose and out through the mouth ten times. Then place a hand or both hands on your heart and begin to visualize, imagine or feel your awareness dropping down from your head into your heart.

Step 6: Set an intention for your experience.

It could be for healing, for self-expression, for freedom, for growth, for fun or play, etc. The intention can be anything that feels right to you in that particular moment. Then visualize placing this intention into your heart.

Step 7: Trust what comes up intuitively.

How do you *want* to move? Notice, trust that and try it out.

Step 8: Notice what stops you.

Notice if fear stops you, or self-consciousness, or perfectionism, or control or anything else that overrides your feeling completely free to move in the way that you want. What is standing between your desire and your ability to act on that desire?

Step 9: Get curious.

Let it be a practice of inquiry – notice what emotions come up and let them be there. They may be joyful emotions, awkward emotions, uncomfortable emotions, ecstatic emotions. Breathe into them deeply. Thank your emotions for providing you with information from your soul that you can use to grow and heal.

Step 10: Resist the urge to edit or critique.

It's not about choreographing the moves from your head, and it doesn't matter what it looks like. Resist the urge to observe yourself with a critical eye or a critical voice that wants to edit what you're doing. When you find this happening, gently shift your attention from your outside awareness back to your inner awareness, paying attention to *how does this feel* instead of *how does this look?*

Step 11: Imagine that there's no way you can do it wrong.

Imagine that every single movement you make, no matter how small or seemingly insignificant, no matter how awkward or natural, is divine perfection in motion. Like stringing words together to pray, you're stringing each movement together in a sacred healing sentence. It's perfect because it feels good, not because it has to look good.

Forgotten HOW to move??

Try this...

- *Jump up and down*
- *Shake each body part separately, then shake everything all at once*
- *Twirl*
- *Bounce from foot to foot*
- *Reach your arms overhead, sway your body and arms like the branches of a tree*
- *Open your heart/chest to the front by opening your arms wide, then open the back of your heart by giving yourself a big hug with both arms*
- *Bounce your heart/chest to the rhythm of the beat*
- *Shimmy your shoulders back and forth, drop them up and down*
- *Bend your knees and bounce your hips, shake your hips side to side*
- *Clap your hands, snap your fingers*
- *Stop and marinate in a moment of stillness, breathe in and out deeply*
- *Lie on the ground and let your body become heavy, feel any heavy feelings inside of you and give them to Mother Earth beneath you as you audibly exhale or sigh*
- *Slowly return to standing*

Repeat these movements or start to move in any way that feels good to you!

Imagine that you're three years old again and you don't even have to think about it, and you don't give a damn as to what it looks like, or what anyone else thinks about you. The music comes on and you just *bounce, move, DANCE.*

Solstice Blessings to you, my friend! However you choose to celebrate between now and the end of December, may it serve as a way to warm your body, open your heart, and infuse your spirit with hope! There is no being on this Earth not touched by the sun or affected by its light – so let our rituals, ceremonies, celebrations – and dancing! – at this time of year remind us of the connection we share with everyone and everything living here together on this planet.

Sending love and healing as you dance your way through this month!

January:
Embracing Quiet

SINCE OUR CALENDAR MARKS this as the official start of a new year, January arrives with an energy of new beginnings. And although we hold each other accountable to that and offer collective support at this time of year for all the new habits we try so hard to begin, if you peel back the *"NEW BEGINNINGS"* overlay that we've put onto January, and pay attention to the energy of the season beneath the expectations, you'll find that we're smack dab in the middle of the dead of winter. And winter...is a time for deep rest, restoration, healing, quiet, solitude, stillness. Not exactly New Year resolution energy, eh? So, don't worry wherever you're at with your New Year's resolutions this month — whether you're well on your way into your new habits, cursing yourself for already screwing up, or just now realizing that you forgot to set any resolutions at all, I have good news. It doesn't matter!

Once spring starts to approach, there will be plenty of opportunities for new beginnings that are more aligned with the seasonal energy that surrounds us. Remember that life has periods of waxing *and* waning, times for growth *and* rest. And it's imperative to honor the periods of rest just as much as we honor the times for growth. Without the rest, we won't have the energy with which to grow.

A Radical Perspective of the New Year

A few years back, I was completely out of commission for the first two weeks of the year when I got sick with Covid right over the new year. And it was another week or two after that before I had my usual amount of energy back. Was there a deeper message in being completely out of commission for most of January? Perhaps it was my enforced reminder about the importance of deep rest.

A radical perspective we can take of the New Year, right? Letting go of all of the expectations to *do, go, change, make, force, create*. And instead, resting into *being*. Knowing that in due time, energy both within and without will begin to shift and nature's new year will be upon us with the Spring Equinox, giving us another chance at making those resolutions – a chance that is more aligned with the incoming "yang" energy of the spring.

And while spring might feel like it's light years away from where we are now in the middle of the winter, there are still other opportunities to set intentions before the Spring Equinox arrives. One of those is the first New Moon of the calendar year. You'll have to google "January new moon" for whatever year you're in to determine the exact date, but it will occur sometime this month. Much like a new year, the energy of the new moon is one of new beginnings, and starting a new cycle. Because it reoccurs once per month, it's always a great time for intention setting whether you're re-committing to resolutions you set at the beginning of the year, or creating new ones altogether.

Aligning with the new moon this month to reflet on the lessons learned from your past year, and to set intentions for your upcoming year, can be an important and useful practice to keep you soul-aligned and walking your highest path. But remember to keep in mind that until the spring equinox in March, we are still in a season of *full yin energy*. That means giving yourself permission to let go of having to force any outcomes or make things happen right now, letting up on your self-expectations, and allowing yourself to rest and just BE.

Be Like Water

So, what can we do at this time of year instead?

1. REST. Know that it's OK to do less. Practice non-doing and allow yourself to just BE. Feeling like you want to hibernate is a perfectly normal reaction to the middle of the winter.

2. LISTEN. To the whispers of your heart and soul speaking to you about what you most need right now. Listen, and then honor those needs. Practice loving, healing acts of soul-care.

3. PLAY AND LAUGH! If you need a reminder about the importance of play, or tools for determining what that looks like in your current adult life, go back to Chapter 8 during the month of October. Remember

that play is a perfect outward expression of non-doing energy!

4. **BE LIKE WATER**, the element associated with the season of winter in Chinese Five Element Theory. Practice honoring the concepts associated with this element by playing around with integrating the characteristics of yin and divine feminine energy into the way you approach and live your life:

   - **FLOW**: Letting life flow. Letting your emotions flow instead of blocking or repressing them.
   - **THE PATH OF LEAST RESISTANCE**: Balancing the masculine/yang energy of force with the feminine/yin energy of receptivity. When water is blocked, it finds a new way around; can you choose to see the obstacles on your path as detours in the right direction?
   - **DIVINE TIMING**: Trusting that everything is unfolding perfectly.

5. **SET INTENTIONS** for the year without feeling that you must *make them happen* right now. We don't give ourselves a lot of credit for having clear vision around what it is we'd like to create. We tend to only give credit when we're physically in action trying to make those things happen. But that's a very exclusively masculine/yang energetic approach, when we could use a lot less energy making those things happen if we first take the time to dream, ponder, and visualize them. Let this be a time for engaging in the feminine/yin energetic half of the

manifesting equation. Discover the clarity that arises when you pause before immediately getting into action. Then use the energy of the New Moon this month to supercharge those intentions by utilizing the following practice!

-JANUARY PRACTICE-

CREATE A POWERFUL VISION
WITH THE NEW MOON

As we greet the new calendar year, it's a natural time to want to honor new beginnings. This year, try something new: sync up with the New Moon to explore two quiet, reflective ways to create a powerful vision for the year ahead while still honoring the deep yin energy of this season.

The practice below offers a fun way to get in touch with the idea of new beginnings, in a way that is more in alignment with the energy of this season: honoring quiet and non-doing, turning inward and reflecting. This practice doesn't require us to go out and get going right away on a bunch of big resolutions. Instead, it's a quiet way to tune in and create a powerful vision for the year ahead.

While the Full Moon seems to get the most attention with its stunning show and reputation for causing heightened emotions and generally loony (lunar) behavior, the New Moon is actually a very powerful time, as well. It is the perfect energy for new beginnings, for setting intentions, for checking in and getting clear on what you really want.

The darkness of the New Moon also has a very similar energy to the darkness of winter – a time to rest without having to rush to put anything into action just yet.

If you're unsure of the date of the New Moon this month, google "January new moon" for whatever year you're currently in to get the exact date. Plan to do your intention setting on that date, or within a day or two on either side, in order to capitalize on the potent energy present at that time. If the New Moon has already happened this month, that's ok. Just set your intentions anyway, and you can always revisit them when the New Moon rolls around again next month!

Practice Part 1:
Four Directions Oracle Card Spread

If you're new to oracle cards, they are a fun and tangible tool for practicing getting in touch with your intuition, that deep inner knowing that is the voice of your soul.

You can find all sorts of beautiful and inspiring decks online or in spiritual or metaphysical shops. If this practice interests you, use your intuition to choose a deck that really speaks to your soul. That applies whether you're buying your first deck, or choosing from stacks of decks you already own. Every time you come to the practice, let your intuition guide you to choose which deck to use that day. I've found over time that some decks are better for certain kinds of questions or topics, but this will probably be different for everyone, so let yourself be guided to what feels right for you.

Each deck will likely come with a guidebook showing all sorts of different card spreads. You can also make up your own, or keep it simple and pick a single card. Play around and have fun with the possibilities! The practice below is one I created for the month of January as a way to do some reflecting on the past year and planning and envisioning for the next.

Select your deck and then follow the process below:

1. **CENTER:**

Take a moment to sit quietly and close your eyes. Take a deep breath in through the nose, and then let it out through the mouth with a sigh as you release any tension in the body. Do this twice more, continuing to let your body relax. Then take three deep breaths, in through the nose and sighing out through the mouth, as you release any chaos in your mind. Then take three more deep breaths in through the nose and out through the mouth, as you release any heaviness in your heart.

2. **CLEAR:**

If you like burning herbs or using incense, this can be a nice time for that as an extra way to clear your energy field, and your deck. Also, it's fun and smells good. Totally optional. You could also simply light a candle or do anything else that feels sacred to you.

3. **CONNECT:**

Pick up your deck and hold it to your heart. Remember that the cards are simply a tool for creating a connection. That might be a deeper connection with yourself, or you could use it as an opportunity to connect with something greater than yourself. The cards themselves aren't magic, they are tools, and tools serve different purposes depending on how you choose to use them. Ask internally to be connected to whatever feels right to you – this could be asking to connect to your spirit guides, your angels, archangels; to your ancestors or loved ones who have passed on; it could be asking to connect with the Universe, the Divine, the Great Mystery, God, or Goddess; it could be asking to connect to the great teachers and ascended masters such as Jesus, Mary Magdalene, Buddha, Quan Yin. The beauty here is that a practice like this – which is called divination – is able to work with any spiritual practice, beliefs, or deities that you have a connection to.

Or you could simply ask to connect with your higher self. This can be a spiritual practice, but you can also approach it from a solely psychological perspective as well, seeing how the message on the card can shift your mental state.

4.   TIPS FOR CHOOSING THE CARDS:
As you're selecting the cards listed in the next step, play around with these various methods and see what you like best. This is a good time to practice using your intuition – do you hear/see/feel/know which cards to choose? You can go about this a few different ways – shuffling the deck until a card sticks out or falls out; cutting the pile wherever it feels right and then choosing the card on top of the bottom half; or spreading all the cards onto the floor or a table and intuitively choosing the one that calls to you or that feels right as you pass your hand over it. If there's another method for choosing cards that you prefer, feel free to use that, too!

5.   ASK:
For this practice, you have four questions to ask and four cards to draw. Create a diamond shape as you lay the cards out one by one, starting with card #1 at the bottom of the diamond.

- **CARD #1:** *What am I releasing into the past year?*

Ask this question, choose a card and then place this card at the bottom of the diamond, representing the direction of "South" and the action of shedding the old.

- **CARD #2:** *What shadow work do I need to look at during this coming year?*

Ask this question, choose a card and then place this card at the left side of the diamond, representing the direction of "West" and the action of going into the darkness.

- **CARD #3:** *What sweetness am I bringing into my life this year?*

Ask this question, choose a card and then place this card at the top of the diamond, representing the direction of "North" and all the good in your life.

- **CARD #4:** *What is the highest outcome for this year?*

Ask this question, choose a card and then place this card at the right side of the diamond, representing the direction of "East" and your highest self.

6. **RECEIVE THE MESSAGES:**

Most oracle decks come with a guidebook that will offer you lots of ways to think about the meaning and message of each card. But before you read the accompanying message in the book, take a moment to check in with your own intuitive knowing. What is the message of each card, according to your own inner wisdom? This is another helpful way to start listening to your intuition. Many of us are likely seeking ways to balance an over-reliance on the logical, rational, masculine left brain, so this is an excellent practice to engage your intuitive, imaginative, creative right brain. Look at the front of each card you've picked, read the words, notice the imagery and symbols, and see what comes up for you. How might this apply to your life, or provide an answer to the question that you've just asked?

After you take a moment to sit with your own interpretation of the meaning of each card, then turn to your guidebook and see what additional messages might be available to you there, as well.

Practice Part 2:
Setting Intentions with the New Moon

Using the information gathered in the Four Directions Oracle Card Spread, set your intentions on or within a few days of the New Moon following the steps below.

Step 1. Breathe Deeply:

Begin by taking ten long, slow, deep breaths in and out of your nose to turn on your Parasympathetic Nervous System. This is the calming system of the body and will shift you out of the chronic fight-or-flight stress state and into rest-and-digest mode, a state of calm relaxation.

Step 2. Reflect & Get Clear:

Look over the messages you received from the Four Directions Oracle Card Spread. What did you resonate with? What stood out to you? What gave you a feeling of excitement, hope or courage? What pieces of you are ready to be released or healed in order to make the space for this? Use this information to help inform your dreams and plans for this coming year. This hopefully helps you to get at some deeper layers of growth and healing that are possible for you. Sometimes it's easy to get into autopilot about what we think we really want. We'll set the same resolutions every year – lose five pounds, eat healthier, exercise more. While those might be worthwhile goals, don't stop at only wishing for the same old things. Allow yourself to dream until you feel an ember of excitement catch inside of you!

Step 3. List Your Intentions:

Using the information gathered from the previous step, make a list of 1-4 intentions you're setting for this year. Keep in mind that more isn't always better, as it can disperse the focus of your energy towards your dreams and goals. You could write something like:

- *"I intend to release the old habit of: (fill in the blank with something inspired by card #1)."*
- Or, *"I vow to be courageous and examine this aspect of myself that I've kept hidden: (fill in the blank with something inspired by card #2)."*
- Or, *"I am grateful and excited for this good thing that I will cultivate more of in my life this year: (fill in the blank with something inspired by card #3)."*
- Or, *"I am joyfully envisioning this highest outcome and intend to do my part to help it manifest: (fill in the blank with something inspired by card #4)."*

Remember, there are no restrictions in how you do this. You can use the oracle cards you drew as inspiration, or not. Create your dreams and intentions for this year in any way that feels right to you. You can wish for anything from the mundane to the extraordinary. Keep in mind that it doesn't mean whatever you write down has to happen NOW; just move through the exercise of getting in touch with the feeling of what you most desire. Ask yourself, if I allowed myself to desire *anything* for this year, what would it be?

Step 4. Visualize and Feel It:

Take a look at your list. Go through each intention and imagine what your life would look like if this were true this year. It's important to FEEL it like it's already happening, even if only for a few brief moments.

Step 5. Identify the First Step:

Now look again at your list of intentions, and pick out one or two that you think could reasonably happen sooner than later. Or, pick out one that REALLY lights you up inside, even if it's huge and won't happen for a while.

Circle the intention that you chose, and then write down your first step, whatever that is for you. Remember, there's no right or wrong way to do this and you're not beholden to this step! The first step doesn't have to be something huge, and it also doesn't have to be something that you do *right now*; you're just getting clear on what that first step might even be.

Step 6. Let it Go:

Yep, this is going to seem counter-intuitive. But this is about having some trust that as long as you do your part in getting really clear about what you want, the universe will do its part to help deliver that. In this instance of co-creation, it's your job to get clear on the *what*, and the universe's job to deliver the *how*.

Keep in mind that sometimes the universe has a better, grander, or different plan in mind than what we envisioned and hoped for, and that's when we can get a little crazy about things not going according to OUR plan. So, stay open to the idea that things may unfold a little differently than you think. This is where that mantra I like to use can also be handy: *everything is unfolding perfectly.* Just remember that this isn't *our* perfect, it's divine perfection.

Step 7. Practice Gratitude:

There's an important step in the equation that we often forget about – gratitude. If we have a relationship with the Divine at all, it tends to be one where we ask for help, but we often forget to say thank you! I like to give a little gratitude in advance, a sign of our trust that good things are already on their way to us now. This can be as simple as closing this practice with the words *thank you!* I also like to say, *"thank you for (insert your specific ask/wish/intention), if this is for the greatest good and highest joy of all concerned."* It helps us remember to keep that spaciousness for things to unfold in the best way possible.

Going Forward

Remember that you can revisit this practice once a month if you'd like, with each monthly New Moon, to keep supercharging your intentions, creating new ones, or letting go of ones that don't feel relevant anymore. When we get to the Spring Equinox in March, we'll have another opportunity to set some intentions as well, to either revisit these or create some brand-new ones.

A New Moon symbolizes a new beginning – so take advantage of this time to reinvent yourself and start anew with a clean slate. Use this time to gather your thoughts and plan for the next chapter. Let this be a time to dig deep and uncover your deepest wishes and dreams – and to send them out into the universe becoming one step closer to seeing them fulfilled.

Happy New Moon wishing! And happy calendar new year! This year, may you use the practices above to honor new beginnings in a way that is more in alignment with the seasonal energy around you. And may you enjoy this time for rest and quiet, for tuning in and doing less.

CHAPTER 12

February: Into the Cocoon

ALTHOUGH WINTER IS OUR TIME for quiet, rest and stillness on the external front, internally this can be a very inspired and creative time. Did you know that bears actually give birth in the middle of the winter? Going against nature's usual plan of new life arriving in the spring or summer, bears typically give birth to their cubs at the end of January or the beginning of February. While bears do mate in the spring during this season of outward growth and activity, their embryos do not start forming until the mother bear enters her den to begin hibernation. As humans, we've been so conditioned to believe that the absence of going and doing equates to being lazy. We compliment people who have a lot of *"get up and go,"* who *"climb the ladder"* and *"seize the day."* We think of hibernating bears as deep in a drooling slumber, busy doing a lot of nothing. And yet, it is this period of deep rest and restoration that actually gives birth to new life.

What can we as humans learn from this fascinating bear phenomenon? That we cannot judge a book by its cover; that what we see with our eyes on the external front is not the entire picture of what's happening inside. That slowing down, turning inward, becoming still and quiet – can be the perfect conditions for new life to spring forth. Not only the perfect conditions, but perhaps the *essential and required* conditions.

A Life-Giving Hibernation

I like to call these periods of time *"into the cocoon, out inspired and aligned."* A few years back, after my usual winter break for the holidays at the end of December, I continued to take a break into early January, and then early January became all of January, and then suddenly it was February. But even though all appeared to be extremely quiet on the external front of my business, the wheels were rolling on the inside. I'd originally taken the break away from the external business activities for some much-needed time to relax, dream, envision, read, nourish, and reconnect with inspiration. I'd been in such an output mode that I knew my cup was running dry and it was time to refill. It was time to switch into input mode, to go into the cocoon. And what I found was that my quiet, externally-disconnected time eventually transformed into a steady stream of inner inspiration and creativity. Nourishing rest became quiet inspiration, which gave way to life-giving creativity.

Though no one could see it with plain eyes, I was hard at work under the radar, which is kind of my favorite place to be, planting the seeds and tilling the soil of what I hoped would be an even better business on the external front. And, as if the universe was giving me a little pat on the back while

I was daring to go against the constraints of society and actually take care of myself – while I sipped my tea and read a book, two beautiful souls were dropped into my lap as clients. Little gifts from the universe as if to say, *"hey, we appreciate you taking the time to do nothing and replenish your soul."* While appearing to do absolutely nothing, I was actually gaining clients, making money, and envisioning a better business for the future.

When is the last time you went into the cocoon, or had a period of hibernation? For how many hours, days, months, years, or decades have you been pushing forward with no period of disconnection from the outside world? How creative, inspired, and aligned can we expect ourselves to be if we never take the time to disconnect from the busyness of the outer world, never stop to check in with our innermost needs and desires?

Permission to Listen to Your Soul

Well, right now I am giving you permission to disconnect! But more importantly, can you give yourself permission? You deserve some much-needed regeneration, and winter is the perfect time of year to do it. When we allow nature to be our teacher, we find we are guided in perfect cyclical fashion through periods of growth and busyness, as well as periods for rest and regeneration. Nature's New Year will soon be upon us next month as we re-enter the season of spring. But before we get ahead of ourselves, let us be sure to take advantage of these last few weeks of winter. This is your time to cocoon. Could you allow yourself a day, a week, a weekend, even a single HOUR to completely disconnect from everything around you – all of the expectations that are placed upon you to do, create, produce, accomplish – and instead take some time to just be?

When you give yourself enough space and quiet, you give yourself the gift of hearing your intuition – that wise soulful voice inside of you that knows just exactly what you need. This voice knows exactly how to take care of you, knows exactly what lights you up with desire, and knows exactly what you're ready to let go of. We can spend lifetimes looking for this voice outside of ourselves, but we will never find it there.

When Slow is Fast

When you allow yourself this time to hibernate, to go into the cocoon, you just might be surprised at how productive this can be. How a slow process can lead to fast results; how total quiet can be incredibly creative; how stillness and rest can fill us with the seeds of new life. This sort of change requires us to attend to our insides – rather than always measuring our worth by our outsides.

Are you, too, craving some much-needed time to relax, dream, vision, read, nourish, and reconnect with inspiration? Are you feeling disconnected from your inner wisdom and the cyclical nature of life? When's the last time you practiced "not-doing?"

The world is a busy place. But sometimes the most radically productive thing to do is to stop, close your eyes and take a deep breath. May you enjoy these last few weeks of winter and feel inspired to go into your cocoon. And may you emerge feeling inspired, aligned, and full of life.

-FEBRUARY PRACTICE-

REFLECTION ON THE JOURNEY
+
A VERY HYGGE CELEBRATION

Congrats! You've just completed one full seasonal cycle of life. Even if your journey with this book isn't over yet, this month, spend some time reflecting on the last year of your life using the reflection questions that follow. And, most importantly, don't forget to celebrate how far you've come!

Part 1: Reflection on the Journey

The first part of this month's practice involves reflecting on the journey you've just been on for the past year, during this last turn of the seasonal wheel. Whether you've been working your way through the practices in this book for the last year, find yourself just beginning your journey here, or are somewhere in the middle, you can still take inventory of the last twelve months of your life. Let this be a time to pause, turn inward, and go into your cocoon.

Think back all the way to March of last year at the very beginning of the spring season, and picture where you were, who you were, what you were doing. So much can change in a single year!

Then get out your journal, allow yourself to reflect on the following questions, and jot down anything that comes to you:

1. *As I reflect over the past year of my life, what changes have taken place – externally, or internally? Where did I begin? Where am I now?*

2. *What are some important things I have learned about myself over the past 12 months?*

3. *If I remember the idea that, "sometimes it's not about changing our lives, sometimes it's about changing the way we experience our lives" - how has the experience of my life shifted? How does my life feel?*

4. *Which practices from the previous months have I found most beneficial? Which practices did I skip that didn't speak to me at the time?*

5. *Which areas of my life have been most affected over this last year? Which areas do I hope might be affected as I begin my next turn around the wheel?*

6. *What can I celebrate that feels like a win, no matter how big or small?*

Part 2: A Very Hygge Celebration!

Then, truly celebrate! Do something incredibly kind, nourishing, and nice for yourself, whether that's an hour to yourself for a long, fancy bath; something beautiful or inspiring to add to your space; or a trip to somewhere you've always wanted to explore. Whatever it is that feels like a treat for you. Because you've earned it.

And because it's February, and you might live in a cold climate like I do, I want to give you the added suggestion of infusing your celebration with the elements of hygge! If you aren't familiar with this concept, you might be wondering, *what the heck is hygge?* Well, I'm so glad you asked because it's a concept I just love.

First off, how do we say this? It's similar to: *hoo-gah.* The Scandinavian word loosely translates to "well-being." But hygge experts agree, hygge is less of an easily definable concept and more of a feeling, perhaps even an emotion. Meik Wiking, the author of *The Little Book of Hygge: Danish Secrets to Happy Living* – which should be a staple in the library of anyone with a fraught relationship to winter, as well as everyone looking to bring a little more coziness and pleasure into their lives regardless of climate – says that:

> "Hygge has been called everything from 'the art of creating intimacy,' 'coziness of the soul,' and 'the absence of annoyance,' to 'taking pleasure from the presence of soothing things,' 'cozy togetherness,'" and the author's personal favorite, "cocoa by candlelight."[63]

In cold climates, we naturally seek out hygge as a way to bring comfort and warmth to our bodies and hearts. It's precisely the fact that our harsh winter weather lacks any natural sense of hygge that we are so drawn to the concept. If you don't live in a cold climate, but you've ever visited one over the holidays and experienced an extra special sense of something-ness, you've likely experienced hygge, too. You might have felt that passing flutter of warmth in your heart, but couldn't quite put your finger on it, didn't exactly have the language to capture the moment. And with its focus on staying in versus going out, small groups, and genuine connection – introverts and sensitive folk rejoice: this one's especially made for you!

Midwesterners in particular have had a stoic reputation for far too long. Deprivation is not hygge at all – it's about being kind to yourself, even treating yourself! This is the stuff that's good for the soul.

Denmark has this concept down pat. Now it's time for the rest of us to step it up and get hygge with it. So let your celebration this month be infused with some key elements of hygge! And don't worry, many elements of hygge can be adapted to any climate. So, even if you live somewhere warm and have no interest in putting on a big furry sweater, you can still infuse your celebration with plenty of the cozy and soul-soothing elements of hygge.

You might...

1. **PUT ON A BIG WARM SWEATER OR THICK COZY SOCKS.** Being cold is the total opposite of a hygge vibe. Get cozy for this celebration!

2. **LIGHT A CANDLE.** Or make a fire. Bring some natural light into this dark time of year.

3. **MAKE YOURSELF A CUP OF TEA, COFFEE, OR HOT CHOCOLATE.** Use an actual ceramic mug without a top so you can wrap your hands around the warmth and watch the steam spirals evaporate off the top.

4. **BECOME PRESENT TO THE MOMENT.** Hygge is more than an outward sense of coziness, it's also a feeling we get inside: it's presence, comfort, gratitude. So, no phones or computers during your hygge celebration. Instead, close your eyes, take a

deep breath, and think of something you're really grateful for.

5. **INVITE A FRIEND.** Hygge is also about togetherness, but in a quality over quantity kind of way. We're so digitally connected in this day and age, and yet we still feel this distinct ache for human connection. Invite a pal to join you and reminisce over a shared memory. Or do something new and fun together. Laugh! Remember that it's not about likes, it's about love.

Wherever you are on your journey…pause and celebrate!

It's important to take this time for celebration because so often, we forget to celebrate the good stuff, to pause and savor our wins before we hurry on along to the next thing. So, pause! Savor. Take it in. You've done a lot of inner work to get to this place, engaging with all these healing practices over the course of an entire year, so reward yourself.

And if you've just started your journey here and haven't engaged with any of the practices yet, or if you're somewhere in the middle, pause anyway! It's a great way to drive home the idea that it's ok to pause, savor a moment, and treat yourself *even if you haven't completed all of your work.*

That alone is a huge act of healing for many of us! Give yourself permission to do something nourishing, fun, enjoyable, playful – and infused with the soul-soothing elements of hygge. Not only is that a reward for the end of a journey, it's an important part of the journey itself!

The End is the Beginning

The Divine Perfection of Nature

Staying busy with our outer lives, we don't always tune in to the subtler energetic effects of the seasons. But nature makes no mistakes – everything exists in a perfect cyclical rhythm with times for growth and abundance, newness and change, as well as times for death and letting go, hunkering down and resting. It is only our wily human minds that try to outsmart the perfect wisdom of nature by refusing, or simply forgetting, to pay attention. Nature only fails when human hands and minds intervene. Nature, untouched, is divine perfection.

What can we learn from this divine perfection of nature?

1. **We can learn to find balance.** We can learn to live fully when it's time to live fully, and to rest deeply

when it's time to rest deeply. And we can learn to honor equal time for both.

2. **We can remember the power of our perception.** In nature there are no true weeds. A weed is only a weed when we decide it is unwanted, or we do not understand it. It is our perception that often determines our reality.

3. **We can learn to slow down.** I had a fascinating conversation with a friend about connecting to the *pace of nature.* When we slow ourselves down to the pace of nature, we find that this is the pace where we naturally experience deep peace, and where we feel connected to everyone and everything. It is the pace where we reconnect with our inner wisdom, and where we can access our body's innate ability to heal.

Slowing Down to the Pace of Nature

And should your mind try to tell you that there's no way you could slow down and still get everything accomplished… remember what the wise Lao Tzu observed: *"Nature does not hurry, yet everything is accomplished."*[64]

It's true. Every year the spring comes and the flowers bloom and life returns, and then the summer arrives in grand whirling abundance, and then perhaps to our dismay, the autumn follows and there is death, there is letting go, and then winter arrives and there is quiet, there is rest. And then the spring comes and life begins again. Every year, in perfect timing, everything is accomplished.

What has happened to our lives that we move so fast we can't feel this pace of divine perfection? That we fill our lives so full to the brim that we can't accomplish everything and instead end up feeling overworked, overburdened, overwhelmed?

Nature calls to all of us. We feel it, we know it. Time and again, when interviewing individuals in personality profiling sessions, I have heard the answer *"being in nature"* as one of the absolute favorite ways that so many of us spend our time – or would like to spend our time. We have a love affair with nature because she offers externally what we can't quite bring ourselves to create within: peace, quiet, healing, connection, an experience of our own divine perfection.

The recent pandemic already presented us with a weird opportunity for slowing down, turning inward, and re-evaluating our lives. Maybe we resisted it – yes, it was totally uncomfortable, often stressful, and super inconvenient – and yet, *could it have served a purpose?* Many of us found ourselves called to a slower pace of life – whether by choice or by force. We had the space suddenly available for quieter, simpler pursuits. We found ourselves with an "opportunity" to drastically restructure our lives – and some of those changes have stuck, whether it's working from home, re-evaluating relationships, or discovering just how much we really did need some downtime.

If we continue to heed this call to slowness, to less *doing* and more *being,* we walk a path forward that can lead us to a beautiful place beyond where we find ourselves now. But, it's also easy to find ourselves getting sucked back into old patterns and habits. To find our inner peace becoming frazzled by the events happening around us; to lose our inner balance as the demands of the world pile on top of us; to start feeling a little blah or heavy as we lose that inner spark of playfulness and fun and joy.

Just know, it's ok. Life happens. And at any given moment, you have the option to stop, assess, and decide – *I deserve to feel better than this.* It's the gift of free will. There is always more than one path available. Yes, our free will has the power to destroy nature, disconnect communities, and drive our bodies and minds to the point of breaking. But our free will can also awaken us to what's truly important in life, can open our hearts so that we can feel the connection and belonging we so desperately long for, can inspire us to stop pushing so hard and instead to slow down.

Anytime you start to feel disconnected from these practices, longing for a sense of balance and peace and joy in your life – take a moment to go outside, or maybe just gaze lovingly through a sunny window if it's freezing out, pay attention to how you feel, and contemplate the following:

> *What would it take in my life to slow down to the pace of nature? What would I have to let go of? What shift inside myself would have to happen?*

Your Upward Spiral of Evolution

Though a book has to have a clear starting and ending place, remember that this isn't a linear journey of point A to point B – it's a circle. And in a circle, there isn't any true starting or ending point. Even more than a circle, we can think of our journey of personal growth and healing as an upward spiral. It's an evolution.

Next month as you enter March, you might have the distinct feeling, *I've been here before.* But in the journey of life, we'll never truly be in the same spot twice. Because you are always changing, you are always evolving. Some people seem to evolve at a faster pace than others, because they've decided to consciously partner with their processes of learning and growing. If you are reading this book, then I imagine that you are one of these people! Dedicated to your conscious evolution. You could read this entire book again, go through all the monthly practices for another year, and get something entirely different from them this time around. So, that's the beauty. No matter where you stand in your journey right now, it's perfect.

May you enjoy the moments of great sweetness and great balance that you create in your life. May you remember the peace and ease that is available to you right here and right now. And may you continue to choose to walk the path of inner transformation, of soul-healing and spirit-dancing, all the days of your life.

AN EARTHLY PRAYER OF GRATITUDE

To Mother Earth and Father Sky,
thank you for holding us so sweetly between the realms of
human and spirit.

To Grandmother Moon and Grandfather Sun,
thank you for illuminating both our darkness and our light.

To the Great Spirit, the Divine Mystery, the God/Goddess
that moves through us all,
thank you for animating our flesh and filling us with life,
so that we may dance with it all.

ACKNOWLEDGEMENTS

Thank you to everyone who has helped make this book possible in both tangible and intangible ways.

First off, I've been blessed to have a few wondrous teachers/mentors on my own journey who have influenced my life in deep ways that feel particularly related to the creation of this book:

Michelle Stimpson, who came into my life years ago agreeing to be my business coach and ended up coaching me on all things life instead. Your influence in my life is palpable. Thank you for appearing when I most needed it, sticking with me through all the starts and stops of sickness, and always making me feel seen and understood. I will always remember, *there's no right way, only my way.*

Michelle Pietrzak-Wegner, who infused my life with all things yin. Yin yoga, the Tao, a deep appreciation for seasonal alignment, a shared love of good tea – these things clicked deep in my soul and influenced my direction in profound ways. Thank you for sharing your wisdom, and your tea.

Amy Wilinski, my shamanic teacher who I found by divine accident. Thank you for always reiterating that the best answers come from simply asking our intuition. As a recovering perfectionist, it was always what I needed to hear.

Amantha Murphy, a true wise woman, who introduced me to my first ecstatic dance experience that absolutely sealed the deal that dance is healing. Thank you for that.

Antonia Dodge, Joel Mark Witt and Dr. Dario Nardi for your fascinating trainings, teachings and research of all things related to personal development and Psychological Type. It is truly soul food for this Ni brain. I didn't know the language my life was missing until I met the cognitive functions. Thank you for making it equally accessible as well as endlessly, wondrously deep.

Thank you to my parents, Carol and Bill Goins, for being huge fans of my actual first book, *Molly's Costume*, that I wrote in elementary school, and for encouraging me to keep writing. Specifically, Mom, thank you for always talking me off the ledge on every single paper I ever had to write from kindergarten through college when I would show up as a stressed and frantic procrastinating perfectionist who had a million ideas and zero ideas and could never figure out how to get started. Dad, thank you for always believing that I would write a book, maybe even before I believed it. You are the most amazing cheerleader and support system a person could ask for. I know you're excitedly awaiting the movie, and the candy, in the front row.

And another HUGE thank you, Mom, for your time and thoughtfulness in proofreading this entire book. I will never forget our rousing discussion of our differing views of swear words and slang. I laughed so fricken hard that my jaw hurt. It was tubular, I'm dead. Thank you!

Thank you to the Buckley siblings, Lauren and Kyle, for seeing something intriguing in me many years ago and wanting to help me out of the sheer goodness of your hearts. Thank you for making me feel seen, for all your help on my business in those early days, and for the notorious and mysterious email that appeared in my inbox simply titled, *what's your goal?* I adore you both, even though I couldn't be helped and fought all your marketing ideas.

Also Lauren, a HUGE thank you for your time in editing all of the cognitive function descriptions in this book. Your *deep, revolutionary, and completely un-bizarre* ideas made them tremendously better! It all goes back to you consciously befriending me in Milwaukee when our paths divinely crossed all those years ago, and immediately introducing me to personality types so that we can endlessly analyze everything for all the days of our lives. Thank you!

Thank you to Alex, Lindsey, Woz, Andrw, Lucy and Tracie of The Tiny Book Course, for sharing your gifts to simplify and demystify what can otherwise feel like an overwhelming endeavor (writing a book!) – especially for this recovering perfectionist. Thank you for always helping to take the pressure off. It was exactly what I needed at just the right time.

To everyone who generously granted permission to share your words, works, and/or stories in this book – a big thank you! (Specifics of works cited found in the End Notes section).

To the handful of dear friends, family, and clients who love nerdy, abstract, intuitive, deep convo as much as I do, who love the mess of working on ourselves and sharing about it – thank you for keeping life interesting and making the world so much sweeter.

To so many other people who have shown me love, support, and friendship over the years, who have inspired me, pushed me, or even triggered me – thank you for contributing in your perfect ways to my own personal growth and evolution. I wouldn't be who I am today without you and this book probably wouldn't exist.

And, last but certainly not least, to Luke, my partner in crime, thank you for swooping in and reminding me of my magic when I least expect it and most need it. Yes, I could have done this journey alone, but it's definitely been more fun with you! Thank you for continually inspiring me with your self-expression, giving me someone to grow with, and always keeping it weird.

Introduction - A Journey of Inner Transformation

1 Quote from a letter written by Carl Jung in 1916.

Jung, Carl. *C.G. Jung Letters, Vol 1: 1906-1950*, edited by Gerhard Adler and Aniela Jaffe. Translated by R.F.C. Hull. New York, Routledge, 2015. First published in London, 1973 by Routledge.

2 Wilinski, Amy. Lecture at the Whispers on the Wind Shamanic Training, Golden Light Healing, Sobieski, WI, 2021. Shared with permission. Learn more at https://goldenlighthealing.net/.

3 Saying attributed to Lao Tzu/Laozi, ancient Chinese Taoist philosopher, credited with writing the *Tao Te Ching* in the 4th century BC. First published in English in 1868.

Chapter 1 - March: Planting Seeds

4 Murphy, Amantha. Lecture at the Ancient Irish Celtic Shamanism Training, Golden Light Healing, Sobieski, WI, March 2022. Shared with permission. Learn more at https://celticsouljourneys.com/.

5 Villoldo, Alberto and Colette Baron-Reid. *The Shaman's Dream Oracle: A 64-Card Deck and Guidebook.* Carlsbad, CA: Hay House, Inc., 2021.

6 Linn, Denise. *Sacred Destiny Oracle: A 52-Card Deck to Discover the Landscape of Your Soul.* Carlsbad, CA: Hay House, Inc., 2019.

7 Hawking, Stephen. "An Earth Day Message from Professor Stephen Hawking and ESA." https://stephenhawkingfoundation.org/an-earth-day-message-from-professor-stephen-hawking-and-esa/. Shared with permission from the Stephen Hawking Foundation.

8 Saying attributed to Lao Tzu/Laozi, ancient Chinese Taoist philosopher, credited with writing the *Tao Te Ching* in the 4th century BC. First published in English in 1868.

9 Basho, Matsuo. 17th century Haiku from Zen master Basho.

10 Saying attributed to Lao Tzu/Laozi, ancient Chinese Taoist philosopher, credited with writing the *Tao Te Ching* in the 4th century BC. First published in English in 1868.

Chapter 2 - April: Spring Cleaning

11 Michaels, Lorne. "A Nonpartisan Message from Governor Sarah Palin and Senator Hillary Clinton." *Saturday Night Live: 34th Season*. New York City: NBC, September 13, 2008.

12 Moss, Robert. *The Three Only Things: Tapping the Power of Dreams, Coincidence & Imagination*. Novato, CA: New World Library, 2007. Reprinted with permission.

13 Murphy, Amantha. *The Way of the Seabhean: An Irish Shamanic Path*. Cork, Ireland: Womancraft Publishing, 2020. Reprinted with permission.

14 Ibid.

Chapter 4 - June: Finding the Sweetness

15 It is interesting to note that this poem is regularly mis-attributed to Kurt Vonnegut; the correct attribution is below:

Thomas, Iain S. "The Fur." *I Wrote This For You: Please Find This*. Kansas City: Andrews McMeel Publishing, 2018. Reprinted with author's permission. Also found at: http://www.iwrotethisforyou.me/2007/08/fur.html

16 The hanging glass mentioned in the story contains an abbreviated version of the quote. The full quote reads as: *"The earth has its music for those who will listen."* It is interesting to note that this quote is regularly mis-attributed to Shakespeare; the correct attribution is from the poetry collection listed below:

Holmes, Reginald Vincent. "The Magic of Sound." *Fireside Fancies*. Ann Arbor, MI: Edwards Brothers, 1955.

17 Boldt, Laurence G. "The Tao of Abundance." Soulful Living website, 1999.
https://soulfulliving.com/tao_of_abundance.htm.

Laurence G. Boldt is also the author of the book of the same name, *The Tao of Abundance: Eight Ancient Principles for Abundant Living*. New York: Penguin Compass, 1999.

Chapter 5 - July: Shining Your Bright Light

18 O'Donnell, Trent (Director/Writer), and Jake Johnson (Writer). *Ride the Eagle*. United States: Decal, 2021.

19 Cain, Susan. *Quiet: The Power of Introverts in a World that Can't Stop Talking*. New York: Crown, 2012.

20 Aron, Elaine N. *The Highly Sensitive Person: How to Thrive When the World Overwhelms You.* New York: Citadel Press, 1996. Revised and updated 2020.

21 Moorjani, Anita. "Discover the Transformative Power of Near-Death Experiences." Virtual presentation via The Shift Network. Accessed July 3, 2022. https://theshiftnetwork.com/. Shared with permission granted by Anita Moorjani's team.

22 Howard Thurman quote shared in the book below written in 1995; date of actual quote assumed 1974.
 Bailie, Gil. "In Gratitude." *Violence Unveiled: Humanity at the Crossroads.* New York: Crossroad Publishing Company, 1995.

23 Jung, Carl. *Psychological Types: Or, The Psychology of Individuation.* Translated by H. Godwyn Baynes. New York: Harcourt, Brace & Company, Inc., 1923. (Original publication 1921 in German).

24 Dr. Nardi has many books, articles and keynotes that draw on his lab research on the neuroscience of personality. Of note, the following:
    Nardi, Dario. *Neuroscience of Personality: Brain Savvy Insights for All Types of People.* Los Angeles: Radiance House, 2011.
    Nardi, Dario. *The Magic Diamond: Jung's 8 Paths for Self-Coaching.* Los Angeles: Radiance House, 2020.

25 Witt, Joel Mark and Antonia Dodge. "The Car Model." *Personality Hacker: Harness the Power of Your Personality*

Type to Transform Your Work, Relationships and Life. Berkeley, CA: Ulysses Press, 2018.

26 Ibid.

27 See note 24 above for a few recommended works by Dr. Dario Nardi.

28 The "hidden personality" is explored in depth in the following work by psychologist Naomi L. Quenk, Ph.D.:

Quenk, Naomi L. *Was that Really Me? How Everyday Stress Brings Out Our Hidden Personality*. Mountain View, CA: Davies-Black Publishing, 2002.

Chapter 6 - August: Slowing Down Time

29 Moss, Robert. *Sidewalk Oracles: Playing with Signs, Symbols, and Synchronicity in Everyday Life*. Novato, CA: New World Library, 2015. Reprinted with permission.

Chapter 7 - September: Discovering True Balance

30 Martin, William. A Path and a Practice: *Using Lao-tzu's Tao Te Ching as a Guide to an Awakened Spiritual Life*. New York: Marlowe & Company, 2005.

31 Vasudev, Jagadish (known: Sadhguru). "Sadhguru's Quotes on Work, Life & Balance." The Isha Foundation. March 12, 2016. https://isha.sadhguru.org/au/en/wisdom/article/sadhgurus -quotes-on-work-life-balance.

32 *Cambridge Academic Content Dictionary*. "Harmony." Cambridge University Press.

https://dictionary.cambridge.org/us/dictionary/english/har
mony.

33 Ibid.

34 *Oxford Languages Dictionary.* "Harmony." Oxford University Press. https://languages.oup.com/google-dictionary-en/.

35 While this quote is widely attributed to Einstein, there is no agreed upon original source. The following quote from a book by Bob Samples may be the original source that has morphed over time: *"Albert Einstein called the intuitive or metaphoric mind a sacred gift. He added that the rational mind was a faithful servant. It is paradoxical that in the context of modern life we have begun to worship the servant and defile the divine."*

Samples, Bob. *The Metaphoric Mind: A Celebration of Creative Consciousness.* Reading, MA: Addison-Wesley Publishing Company, 1976.

36 Martin, William. *A Path and a Practice: Using Lao-tzu's Tao Te Ching as a Guide to an Awakened Spiritual Life.* New York: Marlowe & Company, 2005.

37 The "shadow" is a widely accepted concept as part of Carl Jung's theories of consciousness. The following source is a textbook containing a detailed summary of Jung's work:

Cloninger, Susan C. *Theories of Personality: Understanding Persons,* 3rd Edition. Upper Saddle River, NJ: Prentice-Hall, Inc., 2000.

Chapter 8 - October: Remembering (How) to Play

38 The saying first appeared in writing in James Howell's Proverbs, 1659.

39 *Oxford Languages Dictionary.* "Play." Oxford University Press. https://languages.oup.com/google-dictionary-en/.

40 Sutton-Smith, Brian. *The Ambiguity of Play.* Cambridge: Harvard University Press, 1997.

41 Brown, Stuart. National Institute for Play. https://www.nifplay.org/.

42 Ibid.

43 Jung, Carl. *Psychological Types: Or, The Psychology of Individuation.* Translated by H. Godwyn Baynes. New York: Harcourt, Brace & Company, Inc., 1923.

44 *Oxford Languages Dictionary.* "Rest." Oxford University Press. https://languages.oup.com/google-dictionary-en/.

45 *Oxford Languages Dictionary.* "Relaxation." Oxford University Press. https://languages.oup.com/google-dictionary-en/.

46 Shaw, George Bernard. "George Bernard Shaw Quotes." BrainyQuote/BrainyMedia, Inc. Accessed March 15, 2023. https://www.brainyquote.com/quotes/george_bernard_shaw_120971.

47 Marx, Groucho. "Groucho Marx Quotes." BrainyQuote/BrainyMedia, Inc. Accessed March 15, 2023. https://www.brainyquote.com/quotes/groucho_marx_3800 26.

48 Tolstoy, Leo. *War and Peace*. Translated by Nathan Haskell Dole. 1899.

49 Moorjani, Anita. *Dying to Be Me: My Journey from Cancer, to Near Death, to True Healing*. Carlsbad, CA: Hay House, Inc., 2022.

50 Saying attributed to Lao Tzu/Laozi, ancient Chinese Taoist philosopher, credited with writing the *Tao Te Ching* in the 4th century BC. First published in English in 1868.

51 Turner, Toko-pa. *Belonging: Remembering Ourselves Home*. Salt Spring Island, BC: Her Own Room Press, 2017. Reprinted with permission.

52 Halvorson, Gary (Director) and David Crane, Marta Kauffman, and Brian Buckner (Writers). "The One with the Memorial Service." *Friends: The Complete Ninth Season*. Aired March 13, 2003.

53 Cousins, Norman. "Norman Cousins Quotes." BrainyQuote/BrainyMedia, Inc. Accessed March 15, 2023. https://www.brainyquote.com/quotes/norman_cousins_12 1747.

Chapter 10 - December: Dance Medicine

54 Schieck, Rochelle. Qoya/Qoya Inspired Movement. https://www.qoya.love/. Shared with permission.

55 Gore, Lesley. "It's My Party." Released April 5, 1963. From the album *I'll Cry If I Want To*. New York City: Mercury Records.

56 Rumi, Jalal ad-Din. Rumi: *The Beloved is You* by Shahram Shiva. Rumi Network, 2022. Reprinted with permission from the Rumi Network.

57 *Oxford Languages Dictionary*. "Ecstatic." Oxford University Press. https://languages.oup.com/google-dictionary-en/.

58 Roth, Gabrielle. "Top 14 Gabrielle Roth Quotes." Psy-Minds. Accessed March 24, 2023. https://psy-minds.com/gabrielle-roth-quotes/.

59 Graham, Martha. "Martha Graham Quotes." BrainyQuote/BrainyMedia, Inc. Accessed March 24, 2023. https://www.brainyquote.com/quotes/martha_graham_379056.

60 Rumi, Jalal ad-Din. Rumi: *The Beloved is You* by Shahram Shiva. Rumi Network, 2022. Reprinted with permission from the Rumi Network.

61 De Mille, Agnes. "Agnes de Mille Quotes." BrainyQuote/BrainyMedia, Inc. Accessed March 24, 2023.

https://www.brainyquote.com/quotes/agnes_de_mille_125
667.

62 Japanese proverb with roots in the following song sung at
the famous Awa Dance Festival in Tokushima, Japan: *"The
dancers are fools. The watchers are fools. Both are fools alike
so, why not dance?"*
   "Awa Dance Festival." Wikipedia. Accessed March 24,
2023.
https://en.wikipedia.org/wiki/Awa_Dance_Festival#Song.

Chapter 12 - February: Into the Cocoon

63 Wiking, Meik. *The Little Book of Hygge: Danish Secrets to
Happy Living.* New York: HarperCollins Publishers, 2017.

Final Words - The End is the Beginning

64 Saying attributed to Lao Tzu/Laozi, ancient Chinese
Taoist philosopher, credited with writing the *Tao Te Ching* in
the 4th century BC. First published in English in 1868.

ABOUT THE AUTHOR

ANGELA KITTOCK is a dedicated teacher, healer and guide with nearly two decades of experience weaving together the realms of wellness, personal growth, and spirituality. She is the founder of Moondance Wellness Coaching and the co-creator of Enlightened, Apparently. Her first book, *Soul Healing & Spirit Dancing,* was awarded a 2024 Nautilus Book Award for the category of Inner Prosperity & Right Relationship. She is known for her encouraging and irreverent tone with topics that can otherwise become all too heavy and serious.

Supporting her work as a Spiritual Life and Wellness Coach, Angela is certified as a Yin Yoga Teacher, Holistic Nutrition Consultant, Personality Profiler, is a trained Shamanic Energy Healing Practitioner, and has degrees in Psychology and Women's Studies. Endlessly curious about systems for self-understanding and personal growth, Angela has in particular spent much time studying and training in the Myers-Briggs system of personality and Jungian Psychological Type. For many years she has also facilitated experiential seasonal workshops combining elements of Yin Yoga, Mindfulness Meditation and Gongfu Tea Ceremony. An avid tea drinker, she says she once saw her life purpose summarized succinctly on the paper tag of a teabag: *"lift people up to their potential and higher self."*

Angela is passionate about restoring balance to the individual as well as collectively as a species here on Earth by re-integrating the lost divine feminine, coming into right relationship with our bodies and with nature, and utilizing the path of inner transformation. Her own journey through disease and health led her to become both client and coach for those who find themselves on a similar path seeking better health, deeper meaning, and an experience of peace, joy and a little magic in life. She aligns her life and work by the Moondance motto: *"heal the soul and the body will follow; support the body so the spirit has room to dance."*

Angela lives on a quiet lake in Minnesota with her husband and two beefy pitbulls, Franklin and Elanor.

Learn more at:
enlightenedapparently.com

www.ingramcontent.com/pod-product-compliance
Lightning Source LLC
Chambersburg PA
CBHW051304130726

47987CB00004B/1662